P9-ECZ-004

JOSEPH CONRAD
HIS PHILOSOPHY OF LIFE

JOSEPH CONRAD
HIS PHILOSOPHY OF LIFE

BY

WM. WALLACE BANCROFT, PH.D.

PROFESSOR OF PHILOSOPHY IN URSINUS COLLEGE

HASKELL HOUSE

Publishers of Scholarly Books

NEW YORK

1964

First Published **1933**

HASKELL HOUSE PUBLISHERS LTD.
Publishers of Scarce Scholarly Books
280 LAFAYETTE STREET
NEW YORK, N. Y. 10012

Library of Congress Catalog Card Number: **65-15867**

Haskell House Catalogue Item # **506**

Printed in the United States of America

ACKNOWLEDGMENTS

I AM indebted to my teachers in the Department of Philosophy of the University of Pennsylvania, Dr. Louis W. Flaccus and Dr. Edgar A. Singer, Jr., for their helpful and stimulating criticisms. I wish to acknowledge the constant encouragement afforded me by my colleagues in Ursinus College, Dr. Vernon Tower and Dr. Homer Smith. To Dr. Norman McClure, I owe a debt of gratitude for his helpful suggestions in the reading of the proof.

I wish to express my very great appreciation for the courtesy which the following publishers have extended to me in granting permission to use copyright material:

To the Estate of Joseph Conrad, and James B. Pinker & Son, and to Doubleday, Page & Company, for the quotations from their editions of the works of Joseph Conrad;

To William Heineman, Ltd., London, for the stanza quoted from Swinburne's *Hertha;*

To Houghton Mifflin Company, Boston, for the quotations and references to the works of Ralph Waldo Emerson from their Centenary Edition.

Throughout the preparation of this manuscript, my efforts were made possible through the kindness, encouragement, and coöperation of my aunt, Miss Annie C. Callahan, my gratitude for which no expression can suffice.

WM. WALLACE BANCROFT.

Ursinus College
Collegeville, Pa.

NOTE

In this volume, where references are made to pages in the novels of Joseph Conrad, the page numbers are those of the Editions of Doubleday, Page & Company.

FOREWORD

THESE papers represent the effort to reveal the central principle of the novels of Joseph Conrad, especially from the nucleus of such works as discover it, and to permit these tales from his gifted pen to amplify his complex and un-unified system.

Conrad is an artist, and, for that reason, it is difficult to do justice to him by separating his story-material from the philosophy implied. His novels do not illustrate separately the various aspects of his central theme, nor does any one story portray in complete form a single aspect of it. Throughout the entire range of his thought there is a single theme, too essential to treat compactly, too broad to eliminate an overlapping of treatment that serves to give the synthesis necessary for the meaningful unfoldment of his thought. Each tale, from a point of view, is a fragment of the whole, and each fragment rests upon every other. The difficulty of a logical and classified treatment is apparent from the outset and does justice to the art of Joseph Conrad.

Conrad set forth no "dogma," but his novels attempt to "give the light of his gospel" as he saw it, to describe those "accidents" of common life that best reveal the profound significance of the "solidarity" of human fellowship. Like the true artist, he would move us out of ourselves, creating discontent with the old loves and stagnant contexts, stirring within us the creative mood in order to effect a more significant relation with the wider contexts of life.

In a letter to Edward Noble, 2d of November, 1895, is contained his declaration relative to his purpose: "Everyone must walk in the light of his own heart's gospel. No man's light is good to any of his fellows. That's my creed from beginning to end. That's my view of life—a view that rejects all formulas, dogmas, and principles of other people's making. These are a web of illusions. We are too varied. Another man's truth is only a dismal lie to me."[1]

In another letter to Edward Noble, 28th of October of the same year, is the intimation of his purpose: "Well, that imagination . . . should be used to create human souls: to disclose human hearts—and not to create events that are properly *accidents* only."[2]

True to his artistic purpose, Conrad refused to define his philosophy of life. This is mentioned in a letter to F. N. Doubleday, 2d of June, 1924: "I think that an author who tries to 'explain' is exposing himself to a very great risk—the risk of confessing himself a failure. For a work of art should speak for itself. Yet much could be said on the other side; for it is also clear that a work of art is not a logical demonstration carrying its intention on the face of it."[3]

The difficulty, therefore, of a work of this kind, is simply one of method. The purpose of this volume is to allow Conrad to speak for himself through the medium that he selected for the expression of his purpose. There is no attempt made here to superpose upon his view of life one that is alien to his own. It were easier to classify one's own impression—but that would be sure to violate the principle of justice somewhere.

The following argument is not an exact classification. The overlapping in point of theme prohibits such. Rather, it is an attempt to present in a logical form the *degrees of emphasis,* and to outline these in a manner that may serve to interpret the whole. No outline can offer a substitute for the

[1] Jean-Aubry, G.: *Joseph Conrad, Life and Letters,* New York, Doubleday, Page & Co., 1927, I: 184.
[2] *Ibid.* I: 183.
[3] *Ibid.* II: 344.

works of Conrad, and any treatment of his theme may serve only as a guide, an offering of generalities for the purpose of assisting the reader to discover a deeper and richer meaning in the works of this great comrade of our common life.

The substance of Conrad's works will not yield itself without a struggle. It demands the same effort for its discovery that served to create it. The substance is not there in words, action, story—but rather it is through the consideration of these that somehow it gradually emerges and takes definite form. Its form is life: "To snatch in a moment of courage from the remorseless rush of time, a passing phase of life, is only the beginning of the task. The task approached in tenderness and faith is to hold up unquestionably without choice and without fear the rescued fragments before all eyes in the light of a sincere mood."[4]

---

[4] *The Nigger of the "Narcissus,"* Preface.

CONTENTS

INTRODUCTION

THE physical events portrayed in the novels of Joseph Conrad are but the drapery behind which the intangible forces of the Cosmos meet in conflict with the will and mind of man. Physical man is not the hero in the tale of life, rather the stress is laid upon the heroic will and mind. Life is like the blank canvas upon which the picture gradually assumes meaning, uninterpreted in terms of concrete particulars, but like the landscapes and sea-scapes reflect the value obtained through the schema of our deeper forms of thought. It is the transmutation of experience that blends the parts into an interpretative whole, relates and discovers there a value at once inarticulate, but infinitely significant.

In the lives of the great the moral stress is more apparent, for the "accidents" of their existences have touched the more universal appeal in Church and State, but Conrad deals with the lives of the "small," and often with the seemingly insignificant. The immutable laws of the Cosmos are no respectors of persons, and our author is interested in that moral drama basic to the universal expression of human life. In the case of the small and insignificant, its operation is the more apparent because not obscured by the complexity of externals, nor blurred by imputed greatness. It is the greatness of that *inner life* which is essential, a life from which none can escape, not even those whose capacity and narrowed circumstances forbid the larger external contacts. "I am speaking now," writes Conrad, "of that innermost life, containing the best and the worst that can happen to us in the temperamental depths of our being, where a man indeed must live alone, but need not give up all hope of holding converse with his kind. . . ."[1]

It is this innermost life that Conrad depicts in the novels that fell from his gifted pen. The phases of its appearance are manifold, but the theme is one. That theme forbids chronological consideration. The long period over which certain of his novels extend in the processes of composition; the interruptions in which new tales were penned before old ones were completed; would suggest the meaninglessness of publication dates relative to a classified treatment. From *Almayer's Folly* to *Suspense,* there is not that evolution characteristic of many authors. The play of his mind over the whole maintains a maturity of thought. The deeper significance of the phases of human experience was paramount in every tale that fell from his pen.

In a letter to Richard Curle in July of 1923, Conrad offers a significant statement: "I have always tried to counteract the danger of precise classification, either in the realm of exotism or of the sea; and in the course of years here and there I have had helpful paragraphs and articles in that sense. But they never amounted to much. . . . But the situation is now worth the trouble of special handling. I don't mean on the point of literary appreciation, but simply *classification.* You know how the public mind fastens on externals, on mere facts, such for instance as ships and voyages, without paying attention to any deeper significance they may have."[2]

His stories cannot be separated from his philosophy of life. Razumov, for instance, detached from the scenes of his activity, offers little interpretation. His story-material is like the canvas upon which the picture is painted—it is the

[1] *The Mirror of the Sea* (1926) p. viii.

[2] Jean-Aubry, G.: *Joseph Conrad, Life and Letters,* New York, Doubleday, Page & Co., 1927, II: 320.

necessary support for the symbolization of the artist's dream.

That Conrad is an Idealist whose interest appears centered upon the inner life of man, viewed as the result of his selection of ideas seems apparent. His realism is literary, discovered in his descriptive power and in those bold strokes that carry out the rigid logic of ideas. In a letter to Sir Colvin, 18th of March, 1917, one reads this interesting confession: "Perhaps you won't find it presumption if, after twenty-two years of work, I may say that I have not been very well understood. I have been called a writer of the sea, of the tropics, a descriptive writer, a romantic writer—and also a realist. But as a matter of fact all my concern has been with the 'ideal' value of things, events and people. That and nothing else."[3]

The problem of our author seems to be to discover the highest expression of the laws of the "Infinite Individual"; how to use the tangibles of life to promote that expression, and thereby avoid separation from "Human Solidarity,"[4] which separation is tragic in any form, and renders the finite individual an "outcast."[4]

The implication of Conrad's philosophical principles, as reflected in his novels, suggests not only the Kantian notion of the Moral Law, but Hegel's treatment of "existences and reality," and, somewhat, Bosanquet's "World." On the whole, Conrad represents a form of ethical idealism. The formalistic character of his ethics is modified, as likewise, it is implied in Kant, by a kind of idealistic perfectionism, or Self-Realization.

Before entering upon the detailed exposition of these principles as they are reflected in character and events, it might be well to offer in summary a statement and critique

[3]*Ibid.* II: 185.

[4]Terms in quotation are from Conrad's text.

of Conrad's position, and, for convenience, the four divisions listed below may serve in an arbitrary manner in presenting the related aspects of his single theme. That theme concerns itself with the relation of the individual to the social self, which, in turn, is related to a progressive spiritual achievement as such a phrase as "a *nisus* toward the whole" may connote. As one proceeds through the fascinating dramatization of those relations in the novels of Conrad, the theme becomes simplified, and the manifold of details blend into a harmonious whole.

The terms involved in the discussion seem needful as a background, and, at the same time, are more manifest in meaning at the conclusion. There is not an evolutionary procedure from the simple to the complex in the Conradian treatment, rather the first consideration is as mature in development as are the later ones. In view of this, an overlapping of detail and recapitulation of matter can hardly be avoided. For example, there are three terms, separate in theory, yet one in Conrad's meaning. These are "The Cosmos," "The Moral Law," and "Human Solidarity." Although these terms connote the same conception, the distinction in terms of function is briefly as follows: the Cosmos represents the neutral stuff, or the "immensity of indifference" (Conrad); the Moral Law offers the teleological aspect of the Cosmos in the latter's relation to man; while Human Solidarity (Conrad) is the *concretion* of the Cosmos related to which artificial institutions represent levels of interpretation. These considerations suggest the following logical divisions.

I. The Cosmos and the Moral Law

The Cosmos, as the real, is a kind of neutral stuff out of which man moulds the issue, conditions—all that makes up his own peculiar environment. It would seem to be a potentiality, an undifferentiated that (Bradley), the material for the moulding force of mind and will. Perhaps, it would be in accord with the Conradian cosmology to refer to the Cosmos as "the thing-in-itself" to which man's ideas are related as regulative principles, for the similarity to this Kantian implication is striking. Conrad does not definitely label it; it remains the unknown something that man transmutes into points of partial significance.

This neutral stuff is described through its activity of moral significance. Conrad treats the matter negatively, and indicates how the moral significance is made real to the individual through violence to its principles, and through which its "authority" is defined as *absolute*.

The apparent dualism between the Cosmos and the Moral Law is bridged at points of the transmutation of experience. Whatever the Cosmos is, its activity is of moral import, expressed in laws that execute themselves. The Moral Law is the *value-aspect* of the Cosmos, so it follows that the Cosmos is not to be confused with nature and its mechanical laws, which, for Conrad, always symbolizes his notion of a cosmic order.

The Moral Law, like Kant's Categorical Imperative, is absolute, unconditional, and independent of human ends. Its authority rests upon its own ground. The Fichtean dictum: "Act according to thy own conviction of duty" approaches nearest to the Conradian implication. This *ought* of the Moral Law is expressed through dæmonic whisperings, against which man makes his excuses. This Law has a depressing effect, therefore, upon self-love, having in itself no apparent end nor means for human misuse. The object of one's desires has an end for self—but if such does violence to the principles of the Moral Law, the individual suffers moral degradation which is usually expressed by Conrad by the term "outcast."

II. Existences and Reality

There is an interesting distinction made between existence and reality as such. Reality is represented as a "Ghostly reality" (Conrad) symbolized by the external existences of life, while its meaning lies imbedded within the deep spiritual import of these. Existences are the given materials for ideas, and ideas, in turn, give the characterization of the real. Like the *Narcissus*, a tangible existent, it was not really there as such, but was distributed in the minds of those associated with that ship.

The tragedy in the lives of the characters depicted in the novels is due to the false adhesion between ideas and existences. Witness the cause of the tragedy in "Freya of the Seven Isles" and that of the degradation of Nostromo and Arsat. The term "settled convictions" is employed by Conrad to denote this false adhesion between ideas and existences.

Naturally, there could be little performance that might illustrate the epistomological problems suggested. Conrad assumes, apparently, that life is the result of mental events, for the actor's life is meaningful only in terms of those events of which his behavior is the expression. Further, Conrad would seem to ignore what may be termed the "subjectivistic interpretation," that is, that life is what thinking makes it. Rather the "real life" is that discovered in obedience to the Moral Law. "Consciousness as such" (Kant) seems to mean in Conrad a single Cosmic Order which he terms "Human Solidarity."

III. Negativity

Negativity refers to the moral stress to which every rational individual is subjected. The logic of ideas is *necessary*. It determines the whole utterance of individual existence. Man draws or selects his material from the indifferent Cosmos, and in this "selective and additive processes" (Bosanquet) is discovered the ground of sequence. Man is not left to the fate of a false career, however, for through the sequence is the "*nisus* towards the whole," exhibited through the moral stresses of life. Negativity is necessary to the meaningful contact with the Moral Law, and for conscious inclusion in that wider context. As in *Lord Jim, Victory,* and "The Heart of Darkness," there is manifested the exaltation of real experience in the necessary tragedy of negativity.

What is gained by obedience to the authority of the Moral Law as revealed under moral stress? The gain is a vague triumphant life somewhat analogous to the dispositional goodness of the Kantian notion of "Good Will." Observe Kurtz, in "The Heart of Darkness," and Jim in *Lord Jim* as conspicuous examples. With reference to the first, the gain is self-knowledge; in the second, self-realization. In every case it is, in one form or another, the recognition of the *Good* as against merely a problematic good. Through the negativity of moral stress the Moral Law elevates the dignity of person above the utility of things, and brings man into alignment with the principle of the "best for all." This form of idealistic perfectionism has its value vaguely defined in its own terms. The consideration of what one ought to be is the potential material for the actualization of the social self.

Man can do one of two things—meet the problems of life, for the most part, presented for solution under moral stress, or refuse to yield the self to the larger significance. The second results in moral degradation; the first, contentment and happiness—for "The enigma is only made clear by sacrifice, and the gift of heaven is in the hands of every man."[5]

---

[5] *Tales of Unrest* (1926) p. 176.

IV. Human Solidarity

There is a total spiritual achievement in process toward realization, as yet potential, described in its activity as a *nisus,* and to which Conrad refers by the term "Human Solidarity." The term, in general, refers to the Cosmos as expressed in the Moral Law, and, in particular, connotes the concretion of the Cosmos. It is an un-political, un-national, and a divine and timeless society. Separation from this society results from violation of its principles, and such violation renders the offender an outcast regardless of the integrity of his membership in the political group.

Conrad makes special effort to differentiate this Human Solidarity from artificial institutions, the latter connoting levels of interpretation of the former. For this distinction, see "An Outpost of Progress." The codes of morals represented by artificial institutions offer a vicarious experience of the race. The authority of social institutions, as represented in their codes, approaches that of the Moral Law in general cases, while the range of deviation is greater in particular situations. The whole range of social authority is subjected to the gradual correcting influence of the Moral Law. Artificial institutions represent the cumulative effect of individual experiences, and these are being constantly subjected to variation and modification.

There is, of course, a double aspect revealed in the notion of the finite individual and Human Solidarity. The finite individual is governed and conditioned by the physical scheme of his immediate context, but this immediate context is always *in* the wider context of Human Solidarity. The immediate context forms the background of Conrad's novels, while the relation of that to Human Solidarity offers the real drama in his portrayal of human life.

This apparent dualism is bridged by the fact that the real content of life is given by Human Solidarity. The tangibles, existences, objects—as objects of desire within the immediate context—become meaningless when these are attained in violation of the principles of Human Solidarity. As the Chief Engineer is made to remark in *Nostromo:* ". . . things seem to be worth nothing by what they are in themselves. I begin to believe that the only solid thing about them is the spiritual value which everyone discovers *in his own form of activity.*"[6]

In *Under Western Eyes* and *An Outcast of the Islands,* to cite but two of many examples, there is depicted in each the tragedy of failure to relate the value of objects to the content given by that wider context.

Any deviation from the principles of the Moral Law, and disregard for the interest of the "Infinite Individual," results in moral degradation for the violator. On the other hand, obedience results in self-knowledge, which is knowledge of the good for the greatest number, and which lifts man to the dignity of person though his hands are empty and his tangible possessions are swept away. "Droll thing life is—that mysterious arrangement of merciless logic for a futile purpose. The most you can hope from it is some knowledge of yourself. . . ."[7]

V. Conclusion

The whole gamut of human emotions in the drama of conflict with the wider context of Human Solidarity is the central principle of Conrad's philosophy of life. From that principle there is no deviation in his treatment. The degrees of emphasis are manifold, and several novels appear to portray very special features of this principal theme. "Tomorrow," for example, seems to have been written for the sole purpose of exhibiting a worse tragedy than that dis-

[6] *Nostromo* (1928) p. 318, *Italics, mine.*

[7] *Youth, and Two Other Stories* (1925) p. 150.

played in conflict. Bessie lives a dull and prosaic existence. In her drab life there are no appreciable moral stresses, hence, nothing occurs, nothing is *wrestled* from the indifferent Cosmos, and all is mean and small. Because of the lack of moral stress, Bessie is cut off from the context of meaningful existence.

Again, in spite of ignorance, man is ever conscious of the impulse of cosmic forces, of the "whisperings" of the Moral Law within the deep recesses of his being. This is emphasized in man's excuses and attempts to justify his selfishness. Willems' plea for "just this once" was indicative of his consciousness of deviation from the path of rectitude. In "The Idiots" and *An Outcast of the Islands,* is this notion forcefully presented.

Conrad implies, it would seem, that intellectual capacity and "education" as commonly understood are mere ineffectual trappings if the disposition is not the soil into which their roots extend. Ignorance may be defined as lack of self-knowledge. It does not refer to superficiality of information, but to that of self.

Lastly, "An Outpost of Progress" suggests a special treatment of the difference between artificial institutions and Human Solidarity, while "The End of the Tether" rebukes the anthropomorphic conception of God. In the first, artificial institutions cannot be substituted for the meaning of Human Solidarity, and, in the second, a man-made conception of God cannot take the place of the Authority of the Moral Law.

Self-realization is a result and a complement. There is the merciless logic of one's selective and additive ideas, and there is "the Moral Law within," hence, "the enigma is only made clear by sacrifice, and the gift of heaven is in the hands of every man."

PART I

THE COSMOS

Beside or above me
Nought is there to go;
Love or unlove me,
Unknow me or know,
I am that which unloves me and loves, I am
stricken, and I am the blow.
—SWINBURNE, *Hertha*

I. EXISTENCE AND REALITY

IN *The Nigger of the "Narcissus,"* is painted the picture of the ship upon the lonely sea. The men upon her decks are drawn by the necessity of self-preservation into fellowship. About them stretches the "immensity of indifference," indifference to the value of the lives confined to its keeping as its vastness heaves their little world, now in the quietness of rhythmic swells, now with violence as its storm disturbed surface seems to defy, momentarily the law of controlled peace that subsists, as Wordsworth sang, at the "heart of endless agitation."

Against the background of this unending sea of sameness is the *Narcissus,* a collection of individual worlds. Her freight is an intangible one composed of hopes and fears, truth and falsehood—"an intolerable load of regrets and hopes. On her lived timid truth and audacious lies; and, like the earth, she was unconscious, fair to see—and condemned by men to an ignoble fate."[1] These unseen forces are the material for the drama being enacted upon her rough boards. She is one ship, yet many, with the same monotonous stretch of water about her, yet both ship and sea spelling

[1] *The Nigger of the "Narcissus"* (1918) p. 35.

something individually different to the members of her crew as each translates the meaning of these into terms of his separate world of thought.

The Cosmos is like the sea, indifferent, neutral, potential —out of which man moulds the issues of his individual life. Here is portrayed the notion of the Cosmos and its relation to active life, a relation defined in terms of an immutable law—an actual life of which the perceptual is but the garment and expression of its "ghostly reality," for "Haven't we together and upon the immortal sea, wrung out a meaning for our sinful lives."[2]

The death of the nigger, and the final touches as he slips unwanted into the Unknown, has meaning only in relation to that ghostly reality. "He speaks to our capacity for delight and wonder, to the sense of mystery surrounding our lives; to our sense of pity, and beauty and pain; to the latent feeling of fellowship with all creation—and to the subtle but invincible conviction of solidarity that knits together the loneliness of innumerable hearts to the solidarity in dreams, in joy, in sorrow, in aspiration, in illusions, in hope, in fear, which binds men to each other, which binds together all humanity—the dead to the living, and the living to the unborn."[3]

So the *Narcissus* and its tangible parts is but a picture until the same discovers its interpretation according to the value that each member of the crew wrestles from the immortal sea, with the clash and blending of these in the common life reflected upon her decks. The ship is an "existent," while that wrestled by each man from the dumb Cosmos is *true reality.*

The ship, as those men understood her, was simply not there—she was distributed, as it were, in all the minds re-

[2] *Ibid.* p. 217.
[3] *Ibid.* Preface, viii f.

lated to her. What became of the *Narcissus* when the men abandoned their several tasks; when she docked, and they left her decks, some forever? What occurred when another crew mustered for service upon her boards? Simply another set of mental associations moved in and, in turn, attached these to the tangibles of indifference.

This consideration represented dramatically in this tale offers the implied background for all of Conrad's novels. The Cosmos of indifference becomes concretized in existences, while the real drama is in the form and activity resulting from the moulding of this plastic stuff into actuality through the logic of ideas. Like the unseen forces of mind that are bodied forth in human behavior and action, so is this ghostly reality clothed in flesh by which it is rendered interpretative. "Life is a thing of form," remarked the professor to Miss Haldin in *Under Western Eyes,* "It has its plastic shape and a definite intellectual aspect. The most idealistic conception of love and forbearance must be clothed in flesh as it were before they can be made understandable."[4]

The Cosmos is non-ethical. It offers a background at once indifferent and unordered, against which the consciousness of man, as expressed in his hopes, will, and ambitions, plays a drama of tragic significance. Though man is subject to the same cosmic forces affecting brute existence, he is a spectator who may add his own valuation to experience, and determine his own moral relations. Unlike the brutes that perish, it is his to mould the plastic stuff of ideas into meaningful relations. If his emotional reaction is charitable, so much the gain posited against the negative qualia of the Cosmos. This may be observed in *Victory* in which Heyst and the girl were victims of the enigma of existence. Circumstances or

---

[4] *Under Western Eyes* (1926) p. 106.

existences seem to use each, and, within the limited area of these, they suffered in common with brute life. The one, influenced by the Schopenhauerian pessimism of his father, maintained an attitude of contempt, the other, less thoughtful, but more susceptible, bowed before the fate of that which she seemed powerless to resist. But these very circumstances created situations that served to develop those emotions that elevated them in final triumph as they moulded the neutral material into meaningful relations.

Existences look "solid," but true reality is not in them, being discovered in the spiritual import of these in relation to the innermost life. As the Chief Engineer in *Nostromo,* as already quoted, expressed it, the only solid thing about existences "is the spiritual value which everyone discovers in his own form of activity." It is as Conrad remarks in *Falk* ". . . so difficult is it for our minds, remembering so much, instructed so much, informed of so much, to get in touch with the real actuality at our elbow."[5] In the same work, it may be observed that the differences in life reside, not in the existences, but in man. The captain's ship had the better appearance as compared with the *Diana;* the men on both ships were officers; the sea was the common battling ground for both —yet there was a difference between the two not given in the tangibles against which each contended, but "the ruthless disclosures was in the end left for a man to make; a man strong and elemental enough and driven to unveil some secrets of the sea by the power of a simple and elemental desire."[6]

One's activity is the flesh, so to speak, that embodies the spiritual value of things, and that value alone embraces their meaning. One is reminded of Aristotle's concept of "de-

[5]*Falk,* New York, McClure, Philips & Co., 1903.
[6]*Ibid.* p. 21.

velopment" in which the form and matter discovers a true reality.

Finally, in *The Shadow Line,* the supernatural thing that seemed in the mind of Burns to be the cause of their trouble was not more tangible than the forms against which one always contends—the forms of fear, of jealousy, indignation, ambition. As Conrad remarks in *Chance:* "Each of us arranges the world according to his own notion of the fitness of things."[7] In the same novel, the *Ferndale* had been the home of Anthony, the happy refuge for his servants. After De Barral came aboard, the ship remained the same in tangible parts, but it seemed different in the atmosphere created by the ideas influenced by the "world" of De Barral. One fatal night De Barral committed suicide. The *Ferndale* was not the cause—the sources of that tragedy lie deeper. It was the same plastic stuff yielding the form called forth by the pattern of the unfortunate man's ideas. Existences and reality—the first is the picture, the second, its interpretation.

2. THE CONTENT GIVEN

The interpretation of the picture is found in the world of the individual as furnished by his additive and selective processes of ideas. But that world, again, has its meaning further in the wider context in which it is contained. It is that wider context that gives the content to life, value to objects, and meaning to the personal self. No man can live unto himself, for the very meaning and value of life do not emanate from him but from the social context, which, in turn, is more than a present one. The social context, Human Solidarity, is past, present, and potential.

The *given* is outside of the personal self, for the self finds its meaning only in relation to the outside terms of its own existence. It comes from that "divine society," as the Stoics

[7] *Chance* (1924) p. 289.

referred to it, as distinguished from artificial institutions and social organizations. This "society" represents the "Infinite Individual," which makes possible social organization. Institutions, manners, customs, morals—these are particulars in that great universal represented by the term "Human Solidarity." Morals change with the times, while that universal solidarity of fellowship describes a direction—a "*nisus* towards the whole," the laws of which are immutable and execute themselves.

Some have referred to that content given in terms of *social culture*. Such a phrase illustrates Conrad's implication. Like most of the abstract realities, it seems possible to define it only in terms of its function, for it is a term more simple that those that enter into any definition of it.

If one violates the principles of that relation, one suffers from the recoil and is rendered an outcast, no matter how secure one's relations may be in the political organization with which one is identified.

Ralph Waldo Emerson offers the same point of view and admirably summarizes this notion in the following statement: "Our action is overmastered and characterized above our will by the law of nature. We aim at a petty end quite aside from the public good, but our act arranges itself by irresistible magnetism in a line with the poles of the world."[8]

Desires, aims, and ambitions are created by this very solidarity of fellowship. The tangibles of life have their significance only in these connections of content (Bosanquet). Deprived of the content given by this wider context alluded to, and the tangibles revert, so to speak, to the category of mere cosmic material, losing value and meaning for the individual. As Conrad remarks: ". . . I think that all ambitions are lawful except those which climb upward

[8]Emerson, R. W.: *Essays, First Series,* Centenary Edition, Boston, Houghton Mifflin Co., II: 110.

on the miseries or credulities of mankind. . . . Indeed, as virtue is said to be, such ambitions are their own reward."[9]

Just as money cannot offer a substitute for good breeding, nor intellectual equipment for culture, neither can the values of life find meaning save in relation to the ideal and content given by that wider context. This may be noted in *Under Western Eyes.* Razumov was "outside," as it were, of the benefit of fellowship. To be outside of the circle of his fellows was to lose the combined force sufficient to meet the exigencies of existence. He might gain the prize for his essay, but it was only to receive recognition from a certain group. The value of that reward lay not in tangibles, but in those social valuations which are the intangible assets of life.

The bonds of that Society are so interwoven that no one can escape his part in the pattern of the whole. Razumov recognized the forces against him, not seeming to consider that they were the same working for him. He seemed to forget that the plastic material of his existence was being slowly shaped, not by the logic alone of events, but also by the logic of his own ideational processes. By his one act of betrayal, in order to secure membership within a particular group, he broke the bond necessary to that union. In a word, the content given has its Law by which its meaning is determined, and violence of that Law cannot secure the advantages of that content. "The real significance of crime is in its being a breach of faith with the community of mankind," writes Conrad in *Lord Jim,* and in the same work is this significant sentence: ". . . the fact remains that you must touch your reward with clean hands, lest it turn to dead leaves and thorns in your grasp."[10]

From another aspect, the same matter is revealed in the case of Decound in *Nostromo.* Decound had lost the illusion

---

[9] *A Personal Record* (1926) p. xxii.

[10] *Lord Jim* (1927) pp. 157 and 222, respectively.

of his activity because he detached himself from the context that serves to valuate human action. The very ground of his skepticism, on the other hand, was given by the social fabric that he despised. He thought that his environment was hostile, while it was his self-hood that was unfriendly and unhelpful. The "world" of thought that he audaciously created left him empty and disillusioned, and his escape was gone in the loss of that community of interest upon which he based his peculiar pattern of ideas. In the loneliness of despair he cried out and sought the end in self-destruction. The fascination of externals was lost. He had separated these from the content given.

A further aspect is observed in "The Informer" as representing those who opposed organized society. Mr. X— aimed at the dissolution of society, yet inconsistently accepted and enjoyed its advantages. He failed to see that his deadly aim and thrust at the organization of social institutions was possible only because of the principle of that divine society or wider context that gave content to these and to him. "Organization into families may answer to the need of human nature, but in the last instance it is based on law, and therefore must be something odious and impossible to an anarchist. Does a man of that—of that—persuasion still remain an anarchist when alone, quite alone and going to bed, for instance. Does he lay his head on the pillow, pull his bed clothes over him, and go to sleep with the necessity of the *chambardement general,* as the French slang has it, of the general blow-up always present to his mind. And if so, how can he?"[11]

The anarchist, as this tale further observes, could not permit disorder and lawlessness, represented in treachery and fraud, to exist in his group, for even its secular and temporal bond of opposition depended upon *honor!* Artifi-

[11] *A Set of Six* (1926) p. 75.

cial institutions, as representative of social principles, are not arbitrary, but are levels of interpretation of that Human Solidarity, the dictates of which are inescapable. These institutions may be subjected to correction, but they cannot be abolished since they offer the concretion of the content given. Servin violated the principles of social content and he fell into remorse and destroyed himself. The girl found her ideals shattered and sought retirement. ". . . we exist only in so far as we hang together."[12]

These principles governing Human Solidarity bind all regardless of vows, creeds, sex, and national boundaries. It may seem a cruel law, but in that negative aspect is its very safeguard. The law of fire, to condescend a crude illustration, makes possible its uses. One does not need to extend his hand into the fire, but may use the principle of fire in a more convenient manner. It burns whether misused or made to serve a social purpose. So with the Law that determines the content given. Its very rigidity guarantees the rational organization of social life. It matters little what may be the gesture or social theory, from one point of view, one must obey the dictates of that universal society, or be crushed by its recoil.

It is interesting to note in "The Duel," during the Moscow retreat, that the two unfriendly officers were for the time comrades when cut off from their fellows. The very necessity that had created the bonds of society was felt by these two antagonists when the support of organized society was temporarily withdrawn. The protection of institutions had made possible their personal animosity, but once the support was removed, the felt-need for coöperation persisted. The natural love for his fellows increased in the heart of D'Hubert, and the misanthropy of Feraud was proportionately mitigated.

---

[12] *Lord Jim* (1927) p. 223.

In *The Secret Agent,* the misanthropic professor and the friendly Inspector engaged upon one occasion in conversation. The former's vanity was nourished by the detonator on his person; and he felt superior to the social order that he hated. It was the very content given that made possible his audacity. Though he arbitrarily cut himself off from his fellows, it was the principle of human fellowship that made his detachment meaningful to him. It is observed that the professor's vanity changed to a haunting fear when the Inspector reminded him of the numbers of that order. They parted, the professor bitter and lonely, the Inspector, conscious of his mission and the support of his kind. The professor mistook the particular level of interpretation for the universal order that justified it. His remorse and the Inspector's contentment received their content, respectively, from the same source.

These few instances exhibit the force of Conrad's notion of a universal society which he refers to by the term "Human Solidarity." Society, as the term is commonly employed, is the flesh that actualizes that universal at a given time. Like Spinoza's finite moods, these temporal points in the sweep of universal meaning receive a timeless and eternal aspect. In that sweeping aspect life receives its content, objects their value, and personality its meaning. The drama of human life becomes tragic only when man believes that tangibles or existences are the real objects for his possession alone. Outside of the content given, these lose their significance even though the hand grasps them—for something vanishes when the law of that eternal aspect is violated, and the possessor is left isolated, and the thing grasped, repulsive and unwanted.

In *Lord Jim,* is illustrated the notion in more frank and emphatic terms. Near the close of his life, Jim gradually reunited the broken strands that bound him to his kind.

Through resistence of fear and selfishness, he forced his ideas of peace and unity upon those associated with him, and Jim was rewarded with freedom from the bondage of his own peculiar selfishness. Fear had cut him off from the meaningful relation with the content given, and when those anti-social qualities were sufficiently removed and their forces translated into interest for the welfare of others, he was re-united with his kind and triumphed in that final hour of heroic sacrifice.

3. TRANSMUTATION OF EXPERIENCE

It is through the notion of the transmutation of experience that the alleged cruelty of the Cosmos is removed, and individual responsibility is emphasized. The neutral and indifferent Cosmos and the immutable laws of the logic of ideas, by which the mind gives flesh and form to the plastic material of the former, define the relations of the immediate context of the physical scheme of man's environment to that wider one, the divine society, or Human Solidarity.

The relentless logic of ideas in the processes of transmutation of experience is a means both to peace and misery, for there is no elect child who can put his hand into the fire and remain immuned from the consequences. Permanent reality, represented by the notion of Human Solidarity, is transmuted by the individual in terms that he understands. The power of that transmutation lies within man. Man's freedom rests upon a moral responsibility that is not related to himself, but to his fellowmen, for the unity of life is described in a context of which each individual is part as of a living tissue.

Most of the cruelty and misunderstanding in life are due to the deductions that are made from outward circumstances, and these are related to selfish interests. The logic of life's processes proceed from the inner man. Events follow their natural course, but they have an inward side for individual. Whatever may be one's point of view, one must take the consequences of that principle by which one lives. Perhaps the principles claimed are merely assented to—but one rises or falls, not by assent, but by that which is the result of his own transmutation. Razumov, for example, meditated after his betrayal as follows: "For instance, a man goes out of a room for a walk. Nothing more trivial in appearance . . . He comes back—he has seen perhaps a drunken brute, taken particular notice of the snow on the ground—and behold he is no longer the same man."[13] No one would have noticed anything unusual in the behavior of this Russian student, but within his mind and heart were violence, tragedy, and despair. These resulted from the first step in falsehood that lay "deep in the necessities of existence, in secret fears and half-formed ambitions."[14]

It is the transmutation of experience that gives significance to events for each man—and the law of mind and will seems an ordered thing. Neither misery nor happiness is there, but emerges, one or the other, out of the transmutation of experience by a relentless logic.

Each man has his "Secret Sharer," his other self, the created creature of his transmutation. This secret side of existence haunted Razumov at every turn, in every word and gesture of others. He would retire, and significant are the words of the Councillor Mikulin, "Where to?"

It is life itself that is grave, that every day of life that is subjecting man to the "rush of its infinitesimal suasions." The things seen are but the representative side of that ghostly reality, and if the thing seen blinds the eye to the reality for which it offers the material and the means—then

---

[13] *Under Western Eyes* (1926) p. 59.
[14] *Ibid.* p. 34.

there is no gain yielded, instead, misery and the tragedy of loneliness.

Such a principle cannot be put into a formula, and Conrad, perhaps, had no intention of so doing, but it remains evident that when the principle is recognized that the emphasis is thrown back upon the everyday of life, and to the need of that viewpoint that includes the good of the many, hence, of the one.

The history of the individual is that of his own moral experiences in which the mind and will are either victorious or vanquished. The events of life have their significance in the light of the individual's intellectual aspect, in his particular transmutation of experience. Our world is of our own construction, moulded by our ideas, determined by the habits arising from these.

The world of the individual is not necessarily the real world, nor always the best possible world—for always is there that correcting and modifying force "the Moral Law within."

PART II

THE MORAL LAW

I. THE MORAL LAW AND ITS RELATION TO HUMAN EXPERIENCE

THE Moral Law receives a negative treatment in Conrad, for it is always the logical, universal correcting force of life. The apparent dualism between the Cosmos and the Moral Law has been bridged in the previous discussion of the transmutation of experience.

The activity of the Cosmos in relation to man is of moral import. That activity is expressed in laws that execute themselves. The Categorical Imperative of Kant represents the closest analogy to Conrad's implication. The "world as my idea," resulting from the transmutation of experience, is capable of comparison, revision, and correction. This latter function is effected by the Moral Law. Man is not, therefore, left to the logic of his ideas solely, assuming that these have started upon a false career, for the Moral Law gives the warning—man makes his excuses.

Isolated happenings often give the appearance of chance, but the Cosmos, as far as man's mind is concerned, seems to be without law—for the law is described in the logic of ideas. For instance, one commits a crime and thinks that he escapes the consequences—he may escape that which is his particular formula of consequences—but he cannot escape the consequences of the absolute ruling of the Moral Law. The student of philosophy in the person of Razumov, the Planter of Malata, the cultured yachtsman represented by Travers, and Lingard, the rough unlettered sailor of the sea—all felt the force of that moral power, and those who tried to defeat it, suffered, those who obeyed, triumphed.

Private disappointments cast their shadows across the private landscape of one's individual world—shadows that argue the presence of a Moral Law. What is it that brings those crises into a man's soul, that render life at times insupportable, until his very being cries out in desperation. To regard such negativity as evidence of a cruel destiny, a machine careless and indifferent to man's sacred needs, argues, even in this negative viewpoint, the principle that Conrad attempts to dramatize. Dissatisfaction is nature's urge toward the better. To rest content at any point in the human progress of mind is self-defeat for it is to lose the better that is potentially there. Hence, the principle operating through the dissatisfactions of life is the Moral Law—the cosmic push toward the good.

When one deviates from the path of rectitude, or even in those instances where no apparent fault may be attached to action, where it is simply the loss of ideals, the surprise and rebuke one's action receives points to the universal tendency of reason toward the realization of the good. That tendency is connoted in the difficulties of life, the demand for satisfaction and elimination of wrong. In a word, the Moral Law from this view point, is the reinterpretation of ideals. No one is innately ignorant of this inward operation, this urge toward the better, this correcting force of the Moral Law.

Willems, for example, thought that he might deviate expediently from the path of right principles and return later when his object was accomplished: "He imagined that he could go on afterwards looking at the sunshine, enjoying the shade, breathing in the perfume of flowers. . . . He fancied that nothing would be changed . . . and he was unable to conceive that the moral significance of any act of his could interfere with the very nature of things, could dim the light of the sun, could destroy the perfume of the flowers, the submission of his wife, the smile of the child, the awe-struck respect of Leonard da Souza and of all the Da Souza family."[1] He knew his error and resented the correcting force of the Law because it failed to relate his greed with his fellowmen.

Razumov was crushed by the same Law in his heart-rending experience. He sought the sweet without the bitter and went down into the mire of bitterness until self-realization raised him again, scarred and torn, to the recognition of the forces that were silently working within him.

Trace the events of the life of any one of the many characters that play their tragic rôles across the pages of Conrad's novels, and the absolute force of that inexplicable principle is dramatically and emphatically revealed. It appears as a peculiar force within man, relentless and benevolent, forbidding violence to its social purpose. It is the ground of all that is—the implied judgment in every proposition, the reason for man's excuses, and the cause of both his disappointments and triumphs. It is the relentless logic that defines the *nisus* towards the whole.

To name this moral and absolute power contacted in man's transmutation of experience, to attempt to systematize and label it, is difficult. It denotes and connotes everything. For instance, to judge Lord Jim a coward, to stigmatize Almayer for his folly, to criticize the slave-girl's selfishness—such involves an implied judgment which is based upon this absolute principle. We never criticize another because he is not worse than he is, but because he is not better. It is the principle of harmony that remains and makes possible the recognition of discords.

The accidents of life disclose little, for the *real* life is

[1] *An Outcast of the Islands* (1925) p. 3.

within, following an immutable law of its own, working with man when he works with it, rendering him an outcast when he opposes that larger Self. It appears to have nothing to do with morals or customs, save as these represent levels of interpretation; nothing to do with country, color, race, or time, for these are the particulars of its universal and dateless meaning. To speculate, as attempted, illustrates, but goes beyond Conrad's treatment. Conrad advances no further than to infer the plastic and indifferent form of the Cosmos as moulded by the intellectual aspect of man, through the transmutation of experience. As Conrad writes: ". . . there is . . . a sort of profound and terrifying logic in it, as if it were our imagination alone that could set loose upon us the might of an overwhelming destiny. The imprudence of our thoughts recoils upon our heads."[2]

The law of right, of unselfishness—all that makes for the good—remains the absolute tendency and reality. For the good, there is no penalty—a significant fact in itself. The penalties attached to violation of its principles argue its enduring character. The rose that blooms today in accordance with the law of beauty may wither tomorrow, but we know that the rose has faded because the law of beauty remains.

So there is a power, a something expressed in man's relation to the Moral Law that gives him his content, that gives objects their value, that offers the ground of true freedom, and that secures that end and remains in man's failures as evidence of its supreme authority.

2. THE WARNING OF THE MORAL LAW

In view of the tragedies of human experience, and individual degradation resulting from violence to the principles of the Moral Law, and since the exigencies of life start

---

[2] *Lord Jim* (1927) p. 342.

most of us upon a false career, is Conrad's philosophy of life pessimistic? Such would appear to be incongruous relative to the scheme of life reflected in his novels. His frankness in showing the tragic results of those whose lives have not conformed with the dictates of the Moral Law exhibits rather his courage and unprejudiced outlook than a viewpoint to be construed pessimistically.

"Ignorance of the law excuses no one" expresses even a deeper truth in regard to the Moral Law than in the sphere of legal imperatives, and with quite different implications. The *ought* of the Moral Law expresses itself through dæmonic whisperings, and no one is ignorant of its force. That man has no excuse for failure is emphasized by Conrad without a single exception. This positive assertion against the background of negativity receives its support from the reiterated instances of the warning of the Moral Law. No man is left unwarned to the results of a false career. That he recognizes such warning is evinced in his attempt to justify his action and to offer excuses for his motives. One is reminded of Fichte's dictum: "Act according to thine own conviction of duty," that is to say, to prove a certain act as right may require argument, but to prove that right is wrong against the inner whisperings of the Moral Law is to go against conviction.

Lingard promised to leave his gold to him who would marry his adopted daughter whom he had found in a native prau. She was half-white. Almayer accepted the conditions, and his feelings against marrying one of a different race were appeased by his dream of the gold that such a union promised. Lingard could not live forever, Almayer reasoned, and it would be easy to get rid of a Malay woman after the gold was secured. During the marriage ceremony, Almayer was about to reconsider his move—but he argued against this inner conviction, and married his dream of gold.

It is evident that Almayer was warned by the opposition of his selfishness to his own conviction of duty. During his long and miserable existence, the provocations of the Moral Law were manifold, but Almayer argued and refused to deviate from his fixed course. "Day after day, month after month, year after year, he had been falling, falling, falling; it was a smooth, round, black thing, the black walls had been rushing upwards with wearisome rapidity." In his last defeat he wept, not for the dead Malay, but "over the fate of a white man he knew, a man that fell over a deep precipice and did not die."[3]

One day Nostromo came to Viola's café. Terresa was dying and she had called for him. He was reluctant, and hesitated to see her, for she was frank in her criticisms of him and he resented hearing from her the words that symbolized his own suppressed feelings. The warnings of the Moral Law rebuked his concealed selfishness. Nostromo's vanity, due to his reputation for honesty, was warping his vision, compromising his character. At Terresa's bedside she tormented him for his foolish pride. "Where is the harm of people having need of me?" he proudly asked, though she had not intimated that people needed him. It was his form of argument against the conviction that he felt. "They have turned your head with their praise. . . . Your folly shall betray you into poverty, misery, and starvation . . ."[4] she continued. Her words struck him dumb as he slowly backed out of the room. On his way from the café he tried to brush away the thoughts that she had suggested as though they were tangible things.

The same notion is more subtly dramatized in *Under Western Eyes* when Razumov went ostensibly to secure the release for Haldin. Following his own secret motives,

---

[3]*Almayer's Folly* (1924) p. 99.
[4]*Nostromo* (1928) p. 257.

against his conviction of duty, he repaired in haste to the palace of the Prince that he might betray the friend that had sought his aid. At the house of the General, the suspicion of the latter was, no doubt, aroused by Razumov's attempt to conceal his secret motives. He could not inform the General that Haldin's presence implicated him, but, instead, he must rationalize a false situation for the General in order to make the latter move seem justified. Razumov was conscious of the warning of the Moral Law. Again and again in his career escape was offered, but Razumov argued against his inner convictions until his repeated evasions of the moral warnings stifled his soul. "There are evil moments in every life. A false suggestion enters one's brain and then fear is born—fear of self, fear for one's self."[5]

Jean-Pierre, in "The Idiots" represents the lowest type of intellectual capacity among the characters of Conrad. From this peasant it might be expected that Conrad would allow an exception, but he does not. Twins were born to Jean-Pierre and Suzan and the republican was glad to know that his farm was to have strong sons to care for it. Soon Pierre was cognizant of the uselessness of the children. He hoped that the third would be rational. The third, likewise, was an idiot. Three! this republican and priest-hater finally consented to pay for some masses. When the priest came, Pierre felt that he had compromised his soul, and his turning to this source intensified the feeling of self-blame.

Willems was an ignorant man. One day, trying to escape the monotony of his environment, he explored the several creeks that indented the island. He discovered Aïssa, the daughter of Omar. In secret, thereafter, the two frequently met, though fear and disgust mingled in the heart of Willems at her approach. Each time he left her he resolved

[5] *Under Western Eyes* (1926) p. 379.

never to return, but he lied to Almayer, he lied to himself. He argued that he would go just this once—and then he would never return again to see the savage woman. His little skiff touched the bank. He leaped out in haste and failed to secure it properly, and the means for his return swung out into the creek and disappeared. As he walked up the path, the outcast of the islands saw the meaning of his act. His resolutions, his disgust, and determination to go "just this once" were so many arguments against the warning of the Law that he was constantly violating, and which, finally, after manifold provocation, crushed him.

Renouard, in "The Planter of Malata" was an intelligent man, but one who, like the ignorant outcast, argued against the force of inner convictions. Miss Moorsom exercised an enchanting spell upon him, and in order to secure further opportunities of being in her presence, he took advantage of her quest for her lover by falsifying his own situation. One day after leaving her and returning to his ship, he no longer deceived himself. He resolved not to return. All he had to do was to give the command and his men would make ready and he would be sailing toward his plantation. Against this resolution, born of conviction, he argued and planned to prolong the search for the man he knew was dead in order to keep Miss Moorsom near him. That fatal decision resulted in the loss of Miss Moorsom and his own tragic destruction.

It is in "The Secret Sharer" that Conrad has personified that "other self," our real being that urges us against self-interest and to which we offer excuses for acts of self-love. The difficulties in life, aside from the logical procedure of ideas, lie in the persistent concealment of the "secret sharer." The psychological explanations do not interpret the philosophical conditions in every case. Behavior is external, but motivation finds its answer in the intricate recesses of man's lonely being. What we can touch, we can usually see, but what we feel is alone capable of contacting the deeper significance of moral life.

There was no excuse on the part of the Planter of Malata, nor in the secret arrangements of Cloete in "The Partner," nor in the underground methods of Bernardio in "The Inn of the Two Witches." Each character was conscious of wrong, each offered his own argument against conviction, and each, in adhering to the interest of self lost the value and meaning given by the universal context of life.

Finally, the gold that Peyrol, in *The Rover,* had carried in his waist-coat for so long, his one selfish loot, was discovered after his departure by Arletta and Réal in the bottom of the well. Peyrol had argued with himself about its retention and took every precaution to safeguard it. Why Peyrol [illegible] threw the gold into the well he possibly could not have told. That act needed no argument.

3. THE INABILITY TO ESCAPE SELF

The warnings of the Moral Law are seldom heeded when selfish interest predominates, but, as indicated above, the moral world, like the world of nature, is generous in spite of its rigid logic, ever offering opportunities of fresh points of reversion. The moulding of the plastic material into the flesh of ideas discovers the ground of its own sequence. If these ideas do violence to the relation between the object of desire and Human Solidarity, man must inevitably accept the tragic results.

Ambitions are not wrong save when they rest exclusively upon self-interest, exhibiting the lack of conscious recognition of their value as given by the wider context of human life. "Lo, they have their own reward" is true of ambitions and ideas, proving, in turn, the absolute authority of a principle of moral import.

It is because of the constant operation of the Moral Law and the logic of ideas that man, if he persists upon a false career, must protect the logic of its sequence. Far from the scene of Razumov's betrayal of Haldin, the latter's mother and sister at Geneva were unconsciously becoming instrumental in the further downfall of Razumov. The intimate strands of Human Solidarity were slowly and subtly finding connections of content. When Razumov met Miss Haldin, who thought him the friend of her deceased brother "it nearly suffocated him physically with an emotional reaction of hate and dismay as though her appearance had been a piece of accomplished treachery."[6] He could not escape himself—the interwoven mesh of influences of his self-created world. The difficulty of honoring truth in the first instance increases with constant evasion. The intellectual aspect that gives definiteness to the indifferent Cosmos is composed of the cumulative effect of the selective and additive processes of thought. Sorrow, misery, disappointment—these are not in life as causes but as results, finding, respectively, their actuality according to the inevitable result of the pattern of ideas.

In "Karain," the old war chief is described with dramatic interest. By his side is always an old man, a living part of the chief's equipment. One day the old man died, then "something" out of the black mystery of the past ever haunted Karain. In the tale of unrest that he poured out to his white friends, the old war chief told how long ago white men visited his native shores, and when they departed Pata Matara's sister went with them in the keeping of a Dutchman of flaming red hair. Matara was the ruler then and Karain, the old war chief, his best friend. Together they left their country to seek the Dutchman and the girl, both swearing that they would rid their native land of this curse

[6] *Under Western Eyes* (1926) p. 167.

by slaying both the girl and the white man. Through untold hardships the two natives finally discovered the transgressors. Karain loved the girl, but he swore with Matara that her death and that of white man must be for a propitiation. Matara gave Karain the gun that he carried and bade him to shoot straight at the Dutchman while he, Matara, with his knife would leap upon the girl and slay her. As Matara crept toward the girl and leaped—Karain fired, but aimed, instead at Matara. Back in his native land Karain, now chief, felt the presence of Matara and kept the old man by his side to ward off that evil memory. He could not escape himself. It matters not whether the Malay clothes the force of the principle in superstitious colors, it is the same principle. At sea, on land, a heathen, a student—the same forever holds—betrayal leaves the viper in the soul.

In "The Lagoon," Arsat was conversing with the white man. He loved Diamelen whom he and his brother stole from the land of her birth. On a beach, far from their native shores, they were surprised by her countrymen in the Rajah's praus. Arsat's brother, who had a gun, bade Arsat and Diamelen to flee to the creek and in a canoe that they would find there, to wait for him. Arsat's brother could run as fleet as a deer. In the canoe the two lovers waited. They heard one shot, then two, then three—and they saw Arsat's brother running toward them with the men in close pursuit. Arsat loved his brother, but he feared to lose Diamelen. He heard his brother's call to wait, but Arsat pushed the canoe into the creek. He paddled rapidly away and did not look back.

That was many years ago, Arsat told his white friend. He possessed Diamelen, but the cry of his brother still rang in his ears. Diamelen was dying in his hut far from the land to which they dare not return. The white man listened to the tale of unrest and wondered "at the ever-ready suspicion of evil, the gnawing suspicion that lurks in our hearts, flowed out into the stillness round him—into the stillness profound and dumb, and made it appear untrustworthy and infamous, like the placid and impenetrable mask of an unjustifiable violence."[7]

No one can escape himself. That within him seems to flow out into the stillness and awaken there a voice—is it our own, or but the utterance of that to which our deeds have given language. That voice may be as charmed as the brilliancy of the sun that smiles into the beauty of noonday, or it may seem sinister, like the black and august night against which the threatening lightning plays.

4. SEPARATION

The examples cited have illustrated the relentless logic of ideas, the cumulative effect of additive and selective processes, of nature's warnings, and the inability to escape one's self—that "secret sharer" of personal life.

There is but one Law that man can disobey, and that Law operates whether man chooses to obey or not. Refusal to render obedience to its innate dictates results in *separation* from Human Solidarity. When the Moral Law is violated, consciously or unconsciously, the finite individual becomes *an outcast* in that universal system that serves by inclusion to link his life with infinite significance.

"An outcast" is a term employed by Conrad to connote separation from Human Solidarity. Separation may or may not involve social or political isolation. It may be an obvious separation, as in the case of the Outcast of the islands, or the subtle, intangible form as illustrated in *Typhoon* and in "Il Conde." With Conrad, as a later refer-

[7] *Tales of Unrest* (1926) p. 193.

ence will indicate, disposition is the soul into which the very roots of human experience extend.

In *Typhoon,* the Captain is separated from his fellows, not because of misdeeds, but by an intangible medium of personality. Stubborn, over-confident in himself, unimaginative, and seemingly unsympathetic, this temperamental man cut himself off from his fellows, and from lack of understanding was, in that degree, an outcast. This is instanced in that incident of the Siamese flag and the coming of the Typhoon. When the storm broke, he dealt with the Chinamen in a manner peculiar to his temperament. That temperament prevented him from understanding his men and he was too unimaginative to appreciate his loss.

In "Il Conde" is illustrated a very subtle, but not unfamiliar, form of separation. The narrator of this tale met Il Conde in Naples and enjoyed his unusual refinement and protected existence. There was little in the cultured life of this count that was disturbing. On a second meeting with Il Conde, the narrator of the tale discovered him agitated and depressed.

It appears that Il Conde had met with an unpleasant experience in the park one evening that offended the delicacy of his refined feelings. An audacious young man had robbed him. The count was shocked, not at being robbed, but from the insult offered to the dignity of his person. He felt that the force of his own personality had suffered from this presumptuous act of the thief. He had prided himself unconsciously in the respect that he felt was his due, and when that respect was lacking his whole ordered life was unbalanced. He was not aware of the separation that this pride was creating between him and his fellows.

The same evening, Il Conde repaired to a restaurant and finding his wallet gone, paid the bill with a French piece of gold that he had secretly carried for three years against accident. At the restaurant the young thief witnessed the payment of the coin and approaching Il Conde muttered in his ear: "Ah, so you had some gold on you—you old liar—you old *Bir*-Ba—you *furfante!*" This was the climax and death to that for which the count had lived. Naples became a place of torment and Il Conde fled from the city as from a pestilence.

Conrad exhibits in this tale how the threads of connection between self and the world of Human Solidarity are composed of the stuff of ideas, and if these are woven out of the transmutation of selfish interest, the connection is brittle. Il Conde was kind and humane, but these qualities emerged from his feeling of his right to be so.

A peculiar form of separation is treated in *Falk.* Falk was the owner of a tug, an indispensable contrivance for that river with its shoals and intricate windings. Falk was disliked by everyone, except the niece of Herman who was flattered by the attention of this taciturn vegetarian. Falk was disliked because he shunned everyone and refused to eat meat. One day he unfolded his gruesome tale. Far back in his past the ship upon which he served drifted helplessly in an endless sea. The crew went mad and died one by one save two—Falk and another. These two survivors waited for each other. It was a case of the survival of the fittest. Falk conquered, ate his victim, and was finally rescued. That deed had carried in memory its dire effects upon the disposition of this man, creating peculiarities that cut him off from normal association with his kind.

Conrad does not appear to place any blame upon Falk in the abnormal condition into which he had been placed, but is simply illustrating the fact that anything that severs man from his kind is tragic—a "supreme disaster of loneliness and despair."

In *Victory,* Heyst was separated by his stifled emotions and pessimistic outlook. It was late when he realized that his philosophy of contempt had made him an outcast and shut him off from the enjoyments of life. "Ah, Davidson," said he upon one occasion, "woe to the man whose heart has not learned while young to hope, to love—and to put its trust in life."[8] He had suppressed his emotions in order to escape their effects—but in so doing had not escaped the effect of separation.

Lord Jim separated himself, unconsciously, by a kind of subtle fear that stood between him and his ambitions. His own nature left unsatisfied, he dreamed of great deeds—but his fear remained. After the disaster of the *Patna,* the Court called for facts. Those that were reviewed in that august body were only the visible conditions of Jim's external life, but Jim's mind circled around a series of facts that created the events that led to this disgrace. These were the facts that separated him from his fellows, "that had surged up about him to cut him off from the rest of his kind."[9]

Back of all the examples noted of separation from Human Solidarity is one central theme concerning the cause, namely, the obscuration of the real self by the emphasis one places upon the finite self. That emphasis emanates from selfish interest; in the case of Jim, instilling fear; in that of the Captain, creating peculiarities; with Il Conde, provoking pride.

The connections of content are real, but composed of the shadowy, intangible stuff of ideas. The threads that form these connections are no stronger, no more secure, than the ideas from which they lead.

[8] *Victory* (1915) p. 460.
[9] *Lord Jim* (1927) p. 30 f.

Man must think aright, for thoughts are the substance of true reality. They are forces through which the Moral Law operates. Disappointment and defeats are episodes in the drama of human experience, never motiveless, always purposeful, the conditions by means of which the mind and will are swung out of the orbit of the small into the great sweep of action, significant, social, and therefore—divine.

PART III

NEGATIVITY

1. MORAL STRESS

TRUE knowledge is self-attained and self-tested. It cannot be handed down or transferred to others in its original significance. This is evident from the existence of commentaries, criticisms, and analyses on which men have experienced and felt. If one could preserve the results of experiences, instead of simply the symbols that serve to portray them, one would have, as old Sir Thomas Browne suggested in his *Religio Medici,* the lessons of life, of Justice, and Right in an epitome—and all would read and understand. So with the development of moral life, and the securing of the reward of its offering—such must be wrestled, self-attained, self-tested.

There is a special preparation requisite for every kind of knowledge, and, likewise, for the appreciation of the meaning of experience. The gifts of heaven "are in the hands of every man," but as complements to the struggles of life. In view, therefore, of this purposeful aspect of the Moral Law, no experience is without meaning, no difficulty without its motive. Such is the implication of the term "negativity," as the necessary means to the conscious contact of the Moral Law. The negative aspects of life are *opportunities* for the wrestling from the indifferent Cosmos the reward of triumphant life. Triumphant life is possible only through moral stress.

One is reminded of Wordsworth's Nature with its Law beneath the "sea of endless agitation," and perchance, of Browning's doctrine of "soul-history," the latter of which illustrates those crucial moments when the will stands, as it were, upon the brink between good and evil, to learn, through moral stress, the significance of the one and the meaning of the other.

The triumph of principles is achieved only under moral stress. Without this form of negativity, there could be no development in the proper sense of the term, no recognition of true values, no correction that leads to self-realization.

Moral stress does not imply tragedy. Though its form is determined by those unseen inner relations peculiar to each individual, tragedy results only when the lesson remains unlearned. As already quoted, there is a "sort of profound and terrifying logic in it, as if it were our own imagination alone that could set loose upon us the might of an overwhelming destiny."[1]

Man innately recognizes that "overwhelming destiny." What made those men toil for that old barque, asks Conrad in *Youth,* "it was something in them, something inborn and subtle and everlasting. . . . There was a completeness in it, something solid like a principle, and masterful like an instinct—a disclosure of something secret—of that hidden something, that gift of good and evil that makes racial difference, that shapes the fate of nations."[2]

It was the same principle that invested Lingard in the eyes of Mrs. Travers with worth and power over against her husband's acquired position. When uncouth and unlettered Lingard stood beside her one evening and asked her, after seeing Mr. Travers: "Who is he?" his three words seemed "to scatter her past in the air—like smoke. They robbed all the multitude of mankind of every vestige of importance."[3]

---

[1] *Lord Jim* (1927) p. 223.

[2] *Youth* (1925) p. 29.

[3] *The Rescue* (1926) p. 154.

Likewise, the same principle is illustrated in *The Rover*. It melted the differences between Captain Vincent and Peyrol. There is a worth beneath the surface exceeding those ascribed to external conditions, a worth recognized through the exercise of that universal law. After the capture of the Tartane, Lord Nelson remarked to Captain Vincent: "You don't seem to hate the French, Vincent." "Not that kind, my Lord," replied Vincent, "I detest their political principles and the character of their public men, but your lordship will admit that for courage and determination we could not have found worthier adversaries anywhere on this globe."[4]

That "hidden something," that "gift of good and evil" that "shapes the fate of nations" is the *nisus* towards the whole, an "overwhelming destiny" that knows no defeat.

So in the hands of Conrad, negativity is not an illustration of failures in human experiences, rather examples of the means of triumph. The Moral Law never fails. It is the individual that suffers defeat when he refuses to grasp the significance of trial. Travers was a victim of self-defeat, though he gloried in his acquired achievements. Lingard and Peyrol, though unlettered and untutored, were examples of self-mastery. Perhaps the protected existence of Travers forbade the struggles needful for triumphant expression of character. However, it should be emphasized that Conrad is not taking issue with those of wealth or culture—nor extolling poverty and primitive conditions, but stressing the meaning of difficulties and the motive of struggle. The sacrifice of self requires a self to sacrifice.

Like the great institutions of marriage, of Justice, and law—the principles upon which these rest are strong and universal. They are not in themselves failures, but if men

[4] *The Rover* (1923) p. 295.

are weak, these discover that weakness. Hence, the standard of judgment is not based upon externalities, but upon that principle which triumphs through the moral stresses of life.

The value of moral stress is further emphasized in contrast with the tragedy of defeat and the triumph of principles against the mere gain of tangibles. Since the content of life and valuation of tangibles are given by Human Solidarity, one cannot do violence to those relations without losing the meaning of life. Nostromo obtained the silver, Arsat, the object of his desire, Kurtz, his ivory—but each in violation of those principles, and consequently, the tangible possession became meaningless and without true value.

Kurtz had escaped to Africa from incomparable poverty. He had great plans, great ambitions. He had genius. In Europe his love awaited his return. In Africa Kurtz violated the principles of the Moral Law. His ivory was confiscated, his plans became a vanished dream, and his love waited only to know his memory and her sorrow. Kurtz realized the meaning of his act, glimpsed the truth of that Law just before his body fell into the muddy hole.

The values of life are not discovered in tangibles. "It is the idea," remarked Cantelucci in *Suspense.* Value comes from within, resulting from the triumph over difficulties, in a word from self-realization.

In *The Rover,* Arletta would not have gained the happiness that the companionship of Réal finally offered had she not gone through that strange and heart-rending struggle. Réal struggled against his desires and when he was strong enough to give up the object of his love, he was baptized into a new life, made worthy of her as she had been of him.

In *Victory* the same thought is dramatized. Lena loved Heyst, but she was a disturbing factor to his doctrine of indifference. First, out of pity, the only emotion that Heyst left unsuppressed, he befriended the unfortunate girl of the

Xaniacomo Company. He knew not his love for her until in death she revealed the depth of hers. "Who else could have done this for you?" she whispered. "No one in the world," he answered. "With a terrified and gentle movement, Heyst hastened to slip his arm under her neck. She felt relieved at once of an intolerable weight, and was content to surrender to him the infinite weariness of her tremendous achievement . . . he was ready to lift her up in his arms and take her into the sanctuary of his innermost heart forever! . . . and with that divine radiance on her lips she breathed her last, triumphant, seeking for his glance in the shades of death."[5]

In the strange tale of Hervey in "The Return" is depicted the losing of the meaning of life through greed for position. First, the disturbance of Hervey's inner peace by the leaving of Mrs. Hervey from their ordered home, and secondly, her return which was an enigma for him awaiting solution through moral stress. Under that stress he learned the secret—for "there can be no life without faith and love —faith in the human heart, love of a human being! That touch of grace, whose help once in life is the privilege of the most undeserving, flung open to him the portals of beyond, and in contemplating there the certitude immaterial and precious, he forgot all the meaningless accidents of existence; the bliss of getting, the delight of enjoying all the protean and enticing forms of the cupidity that rules a material world of foolish joys, of contemptible sorrows."[6] That was what he had wanted all his life. The struggle and sacrifice that seemed so enigmatic was clear now in the reward that it brought, for "the enigma is only made clear by sacrifice, and the gift of heaven is in the hands of every man."[7]

---

[5] *Victory* (1915) p. 457.
[6] *Tales of Unrest* (1926) p. 177 f.
[7] *Ibid.* p. 176.

The moral stresses of life are in proportion to the degree of intelligence of those who suffer. The Captain of the *Patna* and his henchmen gained nothing from that terrible experience shared with Lord Jim. Their natures were too coarse to understand, too callous to appreciate its meaning. These men could lie, but did not understand the significance of the lie. But with Jim "there were his fine sensibilities, his fine feelings, his longings, a sort of sublimated idealized selfishness . . . a little coarser nature would not have borne the strain . . . a still coarser one would have remained ignorant and completely uninteresting."[8]

Perhaps the most tragic of all tales is the little uneventful, quiet one called "To-Morrow"; tragic, because there was no appreciable moral stress, therefore no triumph—just a drab, uninteresting existence. The tragedy of life is not in the struggles and sacrifices, "terrific" as they may be, but in what may be lost through self-defeat, resulting either from the recoil of outraged nature, or through ignorance and stifled existence.

Bessie in "To-Morrow," and the old captain Hagberd lived in the persistent hope that the runaway son of the household would return. He would return "tomorrow," was the pivot around which the hopes, ideas, and very lives of these two revolved. Hardships at sea, says Conrad, terrible sufferings in exile, sacrifice and struggles—these excite admiration and pronounce the heroic in him who rises above them—but when there is no moral stress to call forth the fibre of the deeper man, to bring out latent powers of mind and will, the tragedy is supreme! So with Bessie, for "no lofty portals, no terrific inscription of forfeited hopes" characterized her life, and prosaic and uninteresting Bessie "did not understand where she had sinned."[9]

[8] *Lord Jim* (1927) p. 177.
[9] *Falk* (1903) p. 270 ff.

Everyone must live his own life, but the art of living that life is a matter of proficiency. What is it that holds some in fated grasp from the sweep of better things; what is it that causes men to gravitate to the status of the brute? Conrad would appear to answer that the causes are within, for man selects from the content given, and determines the transmutation of his own experience. What we are, that alone can we see, suggests Emerson, but what we are, Conrad might add, has been selected from the same universal stuff, moulded by the same logic, and has its value in relation to the same universal society.

The differences, therefore, among men, is the rational response to that correcting force, the Moral Law, as revealed through moral stress. Individual responsibility and the principle of that Law have meaning in the conscious contact afforded under trial. No one is either immune to the force of the Moral Law, or ignorant of its warnings. The dæmonic whisperings against which man argues, and the attempts to justify his contrary behavior illustrate the force of this relation. It would appear, further, that Conrad rests the whole matter upon disposition. It is the heart and will that are the real heroes, or, as the case may be, the defeated forces of life. The Captain of the *Patna* and his henchmen did not apprehend the situation because of their gross feelings; Bessie lost the significance of her environment because of unaroused emotions; MacWhirr, in the *Typhoon* was cut off from his kind because of temperament; Heyst, Hervey, and Jim were, respectively, triumphant because of the force of those qualities that may be termed dispositional.

Disposition, in its totality, is the fruitage of the transmutation of experience, and, at the same time, the process. It is the result of that transmutation and the determinant of subsequent selective and additive processes. It is the quality through which alone moral stress has any meaning, and, at the same time, the cause of separation. "Warm heart and weak head—that is the riddle; and it is a fact that the bitterest conflicts of the world are carried on in every individual breast capable of feeling and passion."[10]

If the disposition remains unchanged in spite of moral stress the end is tragic. This brings us to the main emphases in Conrad's novels, the cause of tragedy—*disposition.* It is disposition that relates man most intimately with his kind, and offers the ground of negativity and means of self-realization.

Those conditions that prevent the development of the disposition toward triumphant issues are labelled and treated by Conrad as "Settled Convictions," "false adhesion of ideas," "secret fears," and "conceit and ignorance." His term "confession" connotes the "way back" from a false career. These considerations will receive a brief treatment in the following chapters.

2. SETTLED CONVICTIONS

Those who fail to wrestle the gain yielded by the indifferent Cosmos, have only themselves to blame. The Moral Law operates with the material offered and along avenues prepared by the individual pattern of ideas. It is we who "mould the plastic material"; it is our ideas that "set loose upon us the might of an overwhelming destiny." The cause of defeat is one. It may be summed in man's "artful dodges to escape the grim shadow of self-knowledge."[11] These "artful dodges" are manifold in form. Among them is the form that Conrad terms "settled convictions." The term connotes selfishness in some degree. It represents the negative aspect of the transmutation of experience. It is the for-

[10] ***A Set of Six* (1926) p. 161.**
[11] ***Lord Jim* (1927) p. 80.**

mula in which one habitually represents one's own notion of what is significant. When man has launched upon a false career, the ideas associated therewith *crystallize* into settled convictions. These form the shell composed of restricted notions that hide from the individual the real values of life, and which must be broken through before re-contact with "real life" is again possible.

Life progresses through the appropriation of new forms. The static condition of settled convictions is but a relative and false permanency, for only that is permanent that adheres to the principles of the Moral Law, involving, paradoxically enough, constant change and readjustments.

Like the principle of mathematics, life is determined very largely by what is fed to it. Mathematics makes use of figures and symbols for the purpose of obtaining results. Life has a like purpose, and it is the results that count. Meaning is not found here nor there, for there is no finality in life's processes, rather meaning emerges only to be corrected and modified, and to re-emerge, taking on new forms—never the same, but always identified with that principle which we may choose to call the Moral Law.

The static condition of crystallized ideas forbids change, and if the disturbance created by that which we have termed "moral stress" fails to break this self-formed shell, the result is defeat and tragic loneliness.

Lingard lost his fortune, but not his manhood, while Almayer, who builded his career upon his belief in the permanency of wealth, was defeated in its very presence. The conflicts and misunderstandings that appear to arise from man's avarice and lust, emanate in the very first instance from those "settled convictions" born of selfish interest. Life is seen in the color of these crystallized notions and the freedom that gold would seem to buy is made more and more remote as the bondage of those ideas shackles the soul. "Men walk the road of life, the road fenced in by their tastes, prejudices, disdains, or enthusiasms" and the life for them is "strictly defined by those (they) know."[12]

How one pities Almayer, his defeated opportunities due to his settled convictions. When Nina said with heroic composure, "And so Dain is dead," he broke out in violent indignation: "What do you care? You never cared: you saw me struggle, and work, and strive, unmoved; and my suffering you never could see. No, never. You have no heart, and you have no mind, or you would have understood that it was for you, for your happiness I was working. I wanted to be rich; I wanted to get away from here. I wanted to see white men bowing low before the power of your beauty and wealth."[13]

Almayer felt that he had discovered to his daughter the inner meaning of his aims, but he did not know "the crookedness of his ways, the futility of his regrets."[14] He did not see that his marriage to her mother in order to secure Lingard's reputed wealth was now resulting in its logical sequence. "This was his idea of his duty to himself, to his race to his respectable connections; to the whole universe unshaken by this frightful catastrophe of his life."[15] The love of Dain was the only happiness that his dark-skinned daughter had ever known—she could not share her feelings with Almayer, for it was he who did not understand.

The cross purposes in life, the conflicts and fateful accidents are due to the particular formulæ in which these are represented. One follows the relentless logic of one's settled convictions, coloring and interpreting all accidents in the light of these. The whole universe seems to be one of cross purposes and multifarious angles of vision. They intercept,

---

[12] *An Outcast of the Islands* (1925) p. 197.
[13] *Almayer's Folly* (1924) p. 101.
[14] *Ibid.* p. 102.
[15] *Ibid.* p. 192.

mingle, oppose at myriad points. What gives the balance that determines the final issue? That there is a balance, a determinant of ultimate purposes is the implied judgment that makes possible the discernment of the lack of harmony. The lack of harmony is due to the individual's unsuccessful attempts to dodge the revelation of self. That man hates the truth is as certain as he knows it.

Decound regarded these convictions, represented in Nostromo's pride, as the cause of the man's downfall. "It seemed to him that every conviction as soon as it became effective, turned into that form of dementia the gods send upon these they wish to destroy."[16] Nostromo's pride, his refined selfishness, his vanity in his own inestimable reputation was known to himself. It was his form of settled convictions. He knew both the truth of these and hated the revelation of them. When he fell by accident into the possession of the silver, he feared to disclose the missing ingots, not knowing that Decound had used them to weigh down his body beneath the waters of the gulf. This honest man retained the silver to preserve his reputation, and in his fear to lose that reputation he failed to retain it. His settled convictions possessed him, consumed, and burned up his life like "the grip of a merciless nightmare."[17]

Willems, in *An Outcast of the Islands,* had "an instinctive contempt for the honest simplicity of that work which led to nothing he cared for."[18] His bitter end, perhaps one of the most dramatic and tragic in the novels of Conrad, had its inception there. It is always the past to which everything leads forward! Willems thought that he could deviate from the path of honesty without disturbing the relations of life, but his abuse of his trust, his attempts to protect the

---

[16] *Nostromo* (1928) p. 200.
[17] *Ibid.* p. 521.
[18] *An Outcast of the Islands* (1925) p. 17.

logic of his misdeeds, led him to the lowest depths of degradation. In the forest he began to measure his descent: "He wondered at the wickedness of Providence that had made him what he was. . . ."[19]

De Barral illustrates this aspect of selfishness. Flora's form of settled convictions was instilled by her malicious governess. Anthony, on the other hand, was a victim of vanity, vanity of tenderness and generosity. He suffered under the guise of magnanimity, she, from humiliation. "A matter of an uneasy atmosphere disturbed by passion, jealousies, loves, hates, and the trouble of transcendental good intentions, which though ethically valuable, I have no doubt cause often more unhappiness than the plots of the most evil tendency."[20] The drama of life was created by the three separate worlds of these characters, clashing in violent opposition when the three were brought together upon the *Ferndale*.

3. FALSE ADHESION OF IDEAS

Another aspect of the causes of self-defeat is that of false adhesion between one's ideas and existences or objects. It is closely related to settled convictions in which it gradually emerges. A certain position held, a cherished goal upon which one has centered his hopes, attachment to an individual—if any one of these "adhesions" is swept away, life seems empty and meaningless. It may not be save for him to whom the attachment has become fixed.

The difficulty of detachment is always a present one. The value given by Human Solidarity is represented by the tangibles of life. These tangibles and the value attached are two different considerations, the first being the symbol of the latter. One must work in accord with the principles that give that value. When an "object" becomes the center of

[19] *Ibid.* p. 127.

[20] *Chance* (1924) p. 376.

attraction, it is the attachment between the ideas and the object that yields the motive force. Hence, selfishness receives here another aspect in its opposition to self-realization. Further, Conrad has emphasized the ideal-value over against the alleged reality of the physical. Conflicts are not between desires, but between the formulæ in which these are represented, and therefore, real life is possible only where the reality of value is possible—in the world of ideas, for "the motive force of a fixed idea is very great."[21]

When the false adhesion between ideas and objects occur and grow fixed, one strives to protect the issues emanating from these, and likewise, the interest represented by them. When the attachment snaps, the fibre of individual will and mind is tested to the extreme. Winnie, in *The Secret Agent,* whose interest attached itself to her half-witted brother, went mad when that adhesion broke. Ossipon, in the same tale, who disregarded moral laws and defined all in terms of science, sunk by the very force he opposed into despair and madness. The professor, who thought himself strong because he carried enough stuff to send twenty other people into eternity, moved unnoticed, a pest, in the multitude that he feared.

This aspect of moral defeat is well illustrated in "Freya of the Seven Isles." Nelson, brave in physical danger, was a moral coward. He feared the Dutch Authorities and leased the Seven Isles, living there alone with his daughter. Freya loved Jasper Allen. It was a selfish love, appealing to her whim and flattering to her vanity. Allen returned the affection, but always associated his love with his brig, *Bonito.* The brig was to be her home, and he never dissociated the two. Heemskirk, commander of the Dutch gunboat *Neptune,* also visited the island. Old Nelson respected the

[21] *The Rover* (1923) p. 193.

person of Heemskirk because of his association with the "Authorities." Tragedy found its way into these four little worlds of fixed ideas, and the conflicts that ensued arose from the respective false attachments characterizing each.

Heemskirk, in his secret thought, possessed Freya who knew nothing of the claim that she had upon his emotions. She promised to marry Allen, and when the latter reached Singapore he looked upon his brig and thought of the girl of the Seven Isles. The two objects were inseparable for him, and day by day the fixed attachment became stronger and stronger.

One day Allen and Heemskirk revisited the Seven Isles. The blank universe materialized for each according to his respective attachment. When Heemskirk saw Freya and Allen sitting together upon the veranda, he was enraged, for it had an unmistakable meaning for him. Before his departure, Allen asked Freya to go with him—to the brig, her home. She promised to do so on her twenty-first birthday, and he must wait until then. Allen sailed away thinking of her and the brig.

After leaving the Seven Isles later, the infuriated Heemskirk visited the governor at Makassor and was granted permission to capture the brig of Allen. Later, as Allen was homeward bound, the *Neptune* steamed from out of its hiding place and took the *Bonito* in tow. Near the reefs, Heemskirk, who had taken Allen upon the *Neptune,* wrecked the *Bonito,* escaping with his own boat unscathed.

Allen stayed at Makassor, for there he could see the wrecked *Bonito* from the beach. It was there, as he sat alone looking across to the reefs, that Nelson found him and entreated him to leave Makassor and return to Freya. "Come to her! What with!" exclaimed Allen. "If I had been a man I would have carried her off . . . tell her that the day the only thing I had belonged to me in the world perished on this reef I discovered that I had no power over her. . . ."[22]

To her father upon his return to the Seven Isles, Freya, who was ill, said: ". . . perhaps it is true. Yes! I would never allow him any power over me. . . . I've been conceited, headstrong, capricious. I sought my own gratification. I was selfish or afraid."[23]

This tale has frequently been alluded to as an example of Conrad's pessimism. It is not pessimistic, rather, it is forcible in its tragic truth—the tragedy of the false adhesion between objects and ideas. Freya was in love with love, while he, conditioning love's fulfilment in the tangible Bonito, determined himself that tragic result. The story seems cruel, but the destruction of the brig could not have been disastrous without the false adhesion of ideas. Freya might have had—but she failed to save her love because she refused to lose it in unselfish detachment.

4. SECRET FEARS

Another view of moral defeat concerns itself with secret fears. These intertwine themselves with settled convictions and false adhesion to ideas. Old Nelson was in fear of the Dutch Authorities which was the first impulse, as it were, toward the general movement of the events that shattered the lives of his daughter and Jasper Allen. That the last mentioned two are the principal characters in the tale fulfils the conditions of Conrad's philosophy of life, namely, that no one can escape the conditions of the inner self. Nelson's timidity and Heemskirk's cupidity furnished the moral stress for the development of Freya and Allen.

Real life is often missed by the secret misgivings of the individual. Razumov feared, but the uncertainty that he felt

[22] *'Twixt Land and Sea* (1924) p. 236.
[23] *Ibid.* p. 238.

was not in life but in him, for it is "our secret fear, the half-formed ambitions, in the secret confidence combined with a secret mistrust of ourselves, in the love of hope, and the dread of uncertain days."[24] He failed to escape the consequences in the first instance because his secret fears led him into false directions. The intricate web of events following his betrayal were slowly entangling him, creating secret fears that determined his conduct, and which separated him from his kind. His eyes were blinded by that which was shaping his course, seeing only the images conjured by the fears within.

So with the Planter of Malata, the intricate events determined by his deception and falsehood were slowly robbing him of power, for ". . . the moral poison of falsehood has such a decomposing power that Renouard felt his old personality turn to dead dust."[25]

Cruel was the fate of the family of the Dunbars in "The Partner," because of the fears of George. Cloete instigated an intrigue in order to secure a booty. He solicited the aid of George. George failed and brought disgrace to his family and death to his beloved brother. George was not strong enough to decide between his love for his brother and the fear he held for Cloete. The negative forces of life operate with the weakness in individual character, the positive, with the problem that ensues. This distinction is emphasized by Conrad to illustrate that the purpose of moral stress is for development. Moral stress arises from the conflicts between the weaknesses of mind and will and the principles of right, the knowledge of which makes the stress significant. George Dunbar knew where his weakness lay. He argued against the suggestions of Cloete, and after succumbing, argued against the suggestions of conscience. He missed his oppor-

---

[24] *Under Western Eyes* (1926) p. 34.
[25] *Within the Tides* (1925) p. 65.

tunity to strengthen this weak link in the chain. So interwoven is the mesh of human relations that the innocent suffer from the weakness of one member of the family. This emphasizes the dignity of individual responsibility.

The most outstanding example of the devastating effects of secret fears is that given in the strange adventures of Lord Jim. Jim dreamed. Why his dreams did not come true is the subject of this novel. He dreamed of courageous endeavors and heroic adventures. He was always the hero of those dreams, the object of imagined applause. One day on the training ship there was an accident. A man fell overboard. Jim heard the yells, but he did not move. He saw the rush of men, but remained motionless—then suddenly, he made a gesture as if to leap overboard after the unfortunate man, but the captain's hand arrested him: "Too late, youngster," said the captain, and Jim felt the pain of conscious defeat. Here is the first glimpse of that which was back of Jim's cowardice. He dreamed of great deeds—deeds on a large scale: "He saw himself saving people from sinking ships, cutting away masts in a hurricane, swimming through the surf with a line . . . ," but it was always "himself" that he saw doing this, not the act of saving human lives. He heard the applause, but did not feel that spirit that merited it. He centered his own world. When the events offered the opportunity for the exercise of something really great, he argued, then he would not fail. "He knew the magic monotony of existence . . . and the prosaic severity of the daily task that gives bread—but whose only reward is in the *perfect love of work*. This reward eluded him."[26]

Before the disaster of the *Patna,* Jim saw a small portion of the bulkhead bulging. He knew the meaning of that, and he thought of the eight hundred people aboard. He did not rush to report his finding—he stood there motionless as he

[26] *Lord Jim* (1927) p. 10, *Italics, mine.*

had acted under similar situations before. He stood waiting for the burst and the flood. "He was not afraid . . . not of death . . . he was afraid of the emergency . . . I suspect he wanted to die without added terrors . . . the desire of peace waxes stronger as hope declines, till at last it conquers the very desire of life."[27] It was the fear of drawing attention to himself that paralyzed every moment of this applause-loving man!

As Jim stood there on the deck—waiting, he saw the captain and his henchmen struggling like mad men with a boat, the only boat, to get it loose before the ship listed, to get it free before the mob of eight hundred people were aware of the danger and would scramble for that single boat. When the little boat was finally loosed and in the water, Jim jumped. He did not know why, but when he found himself in the boat with its cowardly occupants he knew again the pain of conscious defeat.

In the darkness of the night the lights of the ship went out, and occupants of the little boat thought that the *Patna* had sunk. Jim wanted to jump and swim to the place where he believed that she had gone down. It must be his grave as a propitiation for his cowardice—but he remained motionless.

In the morning they were picked up and brought ashore. They learned that the *Patna* had not sunk, but had been sighted and towed to shore with its cargo of eight hundred people. The captain and his men fled, but Jim was detained to explain. The superficial *how* was explained before the judges, but the fundamental *why* tormented the heart of Lord Jim.

Secret fears construed out of the blackness of the night must be eradicated, removing the uncertainty from within,

---

[27] *Ibid.* p. 88.

so that one, like the proud swimmer in the "Secret Sharer," may strike out boldly for a new destiny.

5. CONCEIT AND IGNORANCE

"Every mental state, even madness, has its equilibrium based upon self-esteem."[28] Self-esteem, that innate sense of personal dignity, is inescapable. No rational individual is immune to the desire for self-esteem. It is the ground of respect and of madness alike, the principle that relates to social advantages as well as to the material for conceit and ignorance. It underlies all emotional expression.

That the principle of self-esteem is inescapable is illustrated even in those who claim to care nothing for the opinions of others as these relate to their persons, for such usually desire to be esteemed for not caring.

The purpose of the Moral Law is to elevate the dignity of person above the utility of things. When this sense of personal dignity is translated into forms of vanity and conceit, it not only connotes a form of ignorance, but creates a separation between the individual and his potential triumph.

In the inner life of man the soul dwells alone—yet not alone, for through the contact with the principles that valuate life, man is brought into fellowship with all. Differences of circumstances, racial differences, conventional differentiations, these are but surface discriminations, while beneath this "sea of endless agitation" is the calm law of moral purpose as the ground of all distinctions.

When the sense of personal dignity degenerates into conceit, there is expressed another aspect of selfishness, separating the individual from his kind.

When Razumov walked the streets after his unsuccessful errand to the home of the drunken driver, and he felt his

[28] *Falk* (1903) p. 242.

inability to tolerate Haldin's presence, why did he not return at once to his rooms, confess that which would have been weakness in the eyes of Haldin, but strength in his own, and bid the anarchist to seek succor elsewhere? Why, indeed? Perhaps the answer is inarticulate, but Conrad has employed naturally enough the processes of thought here to indicate that self-esteem was the ground of his action, fear to do violence to his own conception of personal dignity.

This innate sense of personal dignity expresses itself according to what is fed to it. It may be fixed through settled convictions, restricted by secret fears; but in all—it remains the ground of emotional action.

The moral significance of this innate sense of personal dignity is discovered in its relation to the Infinite Individual as connoted in the term "Human Solidarity." It is the bond that unites humanity in universal understanding. It is the sense, so to speak, through which the Moral Law operates and touches the core of the deepest recesses of human feeling. It is at once the most dangerous and at the same time the greatest blessing in the form of heaven's gifts. Though the violation of this sense renders man an agent in his own downfall and an outcast in that "society" in which alone his real triumph is possible, it affords, on the other hand, through proper relation, man's elevation above the utility of things, and renders him instrumental in becoming what he ought to be.

Just as the solidarity of universal fellowship gives the real content to life, so is the content of true individuality drawn from the same source. When the tangibles are related to self-interest, though possessed, they become meaningless and empty, so when that personal esteem becomes, through self-interest, a form of vanity and conceit, the individual becomes in personality superficial and empty. So it was with Renouard when his self-interest corroded the finer qualities of his character and "he felt his old personality turn to dead dust."[29]

Nostromo was efficient, trustworthy, and intelligent—but these fine qualities became a form of conceit. Decound wondered if Nostromo could be trusted "when this man was made incorruptible by his enormous vanity, that finished form of egoism which can take on the aspect of every virtue."[30] The ritual of life may not always reveal the spirit of the devotee. Nostromo was growing rich. He dare not disclose the source of his wealth. This humiliated him. He lost "his peace, the genuineness of all his qualities was destroyed."[31] The relation of his "need to others" became a form of a need to himself, obliterating the real value of human qualities and resulting in self-defeat.

In "The Return," Mr. and Mrs. Hervey were "unable to look at a fact, a sentiment, a principle, or a belief otherwise than in the light of their own dignity, of their own glorification, of their own advantage."[32] This gentleman of refinement and ordered living saw not the "reality at his elbow." His vanity blunted his finer sensibilities, enslaving him in a bondage of his own making.

Conceit is a form of ignorance, for ignorance is with Conrad any degree of lack of self-knowledge. Hervey, the man of proper conventions, Travers, the wealthy yachtman, Razumov, the student of philosophy—these descriptions delineate only points of recognition, associated environment of external circumstances—while each one suffered from ignorance.

In view of conventional distinctions, Travers and Lingard in *The Rescue* offer extreme contrasts, but, strangely enough, Conrad portrays the cultured Travers as an ignorant indi-

[29]*Within the Tides* (1925) p. 65.
[30]*Nostromo* (1928) p. 300.
[31]*Ibid.* p. 523.
[32]*Tales of Unrest* (1926) p. 123.

vidual, and untutored Lingard as one in possession of that "which is a gift and not an acquisition, and, therefore, more permanently enduring."[33] Travers did not see the real drama that was being enacted before his very eyes. He did not understand Mrs. Travers and turned from Lingard unimpressed. Referring to the unkind reception tendered him by Mr. Travers, Lingard said to Mrs. Travers: "No! I suppose I didn't look enough of a gentleman. . . . Yet I know what a gentleman is . . . I chummed with them—yes—on gold fields and in other places where a man has got to show the stuff that's in him. . . . And I know what a gentleman would do. . . . Wouldn't he keep his word wherever given?"[34] He possessed those enduring and permanent qualities resulting from self-attained and self-tested experience, while Travers rested satisfied in the achievements which conventions had pronounced good, and of which his own spirit found sufficient reason to be proud.

All infractions of these principles that concern social relations in the universal sense are punishable. Perhaps the real tragedy in the life of Jean-Pierre was due to gross ignorance. He could not discern the difference between "the plants that give life and those that give death."[35] But even with Jean-Pierre there were moments of self-revelation. When he, a priest-hater, acceded reluctantly to his wife's request for some masses, he "felt like a man who had sold his soul."

Willems was ignorant. "He experienced that irresistible impulse to impart information which is inseparable from gross ignorance. There is always some one thing which the ignorant man knows and that thing is the only thing worth knowing; it fills the ignorant man's universe. Willems knew

[33] *The Nigger of the "Narcissus"* (1918) p. viii.
[34] *The Rescue* (1926) p. 164.
[35] *Tales of Unrest* (1926) p. 63.

all about himself."[36] Here is offered a distinction between knowledge about self and self-knowledge, for it is not the intellect, after all, that makes distinctions, but the heart, and the heart lives on what is fed to it. The "heart" has its relation to the play of those forces that are severally called selfishness, conceit, false ambitions—and it is these that rob life of its sweet mystery, and blur its reflection of infinite significance, tainting the mind that was made to respond to its deeper calls, and veiling the values of real life that it would discover. These men, Willems and Jean-Pierre were "not, of course, able to discern clearly the causes of (their) misery, but there are none so ignorant as not to know suffering, none so simple as not to feel and suffer from the shock of warring impulses."[37]

The cause of defeat, again, is always within and not in circumstances. The latter offer only episodes for moral action. Man is without excuse since he attempts to justify himself against these "warring impulses," and is always aware of his own self-interest which has its ground in the interest of many.

Conrad extends his treatment of the dispositional character of life to the field of education and mental equipment. He argues, as implied, that culture, education, intellectual equipment sink into ineffectual trappings when the disposition is not the soil into which their roots extend. Knowledge rests upon character. Let him be ever so well versed in the technical aspects of learning and remain infantile in disposition, and he has missed the deepest aspect of culture.

This distinction between equipment and disposition Conrad illustrates in the carpenter who, while making a box, may be mad and think himself the king of Siam, but who will nevertheless make a sane box![38]

---

[36] *An Outcast of the Islands* (1925) p. 5 f.
[37] *Ibid.* p. 129.
[38] *The Shadow Line* (1915) p. 149.

Education, like ignorance, relates to what the individual *is*, rather than to what he can or cannot do. Ignorance, like conceit, is a quality of self. The student of philosophy, the well informed yachtsman, and the cultured Il Conde—these may be ignorant if they fail to rationalize the relation between self-esteem and Human Solidarity, for ignorance and conceit represent lack of self-knowledge. They express those "artful dodges to escape from the grim shadow of self-knowledge."

6. CONFESSION

Man can do one of two things, "stand up to his bad luck, to his mistakes, to his conscience,"[39] and meet the problems of life presented for solution under moral stress; or refuse to yield to the larger interests, and, like the Planter of Malata, find himself isolated, the finer qualities of character corroding from the "moral poison" of a false life. "For in the path of rectitude lies true happiness."[40]

As Conrad reiterates, one is always conscious of deviation from the "path of rectitude." The efforts to evade the issues of self-knowledge, the resolution of "just this once," argue the moral force working within.

That which makes for fulfillment of the happiness and welfare of the greatest number can alone justify human behavior. Hypothetical categories of personal ambitions have ends which may, or may not, furnish the motive power that enhances the interest of the Infinite Individual, while the Categorical Imperative of the Moral Law has its Kantian application in the Conradian ethic. For Conrad, as with Kant, this Imperative has no end that can be misused, for its end is dispositionally goodness.

To attain dispositional goodness that justifies existence

[39] *The Shadow Line* (1915) p. 194.

[40] Jean-Aubry, G.: *Joseph Conrad, Life and Letters,* New York, Doubleday, Page & Co., 1927, I: 85.

and unites one with his fellows in the society of universal values, moral stress is the necessary negativity. Without it one, like Bessie in "To-Morrow," may not know wherein one has sinned. Moral stress furnishes the opportunities for wrestling the gain offered by the indifferent Cosmos, and subtle are the self-created obstructions that hinder its reception, ranging from temperament to gross criminal action.

The Moral Law acts whether obeyed or not. These forms and aspects of self-defeat mentioned in the above given treatments "betray" the individual into misery and despair. Once launched upon a false career, the motive force is determined by expediency, and soon, like Willems one bends his genius to the effort of not being found out. Such, likewise, was the governing motive in the early career of Razumov: "I must be cautious," he said as the intricate web of his own weaving entangled him and "the choking fumes of falsehood had taken him by the throat."[41]

The way back from a false career is to "undo the evil" and "betray oneself back into truth and peace." This involves the supreme heroism of mind and will. The self has been cut off from normal relations by the false world that it has created. To break away from such a condition means *self-exposure,* it means the expression of the deepest kind of courage. The evil done by those false relations must be undone, and though one may stand condemned by his fellows, his willingness to so stand can alone discover that inward peace and that truth which reunites him with his kind. Such is "Confession."

Confession is more than recognition of deviation from the path of rectitude, for such recognition is never absent as cautiousness, pretence, and falsehood well argue. It is more than verbal acknowledgment of wrong, for such may be

[41]*Under Western Eyes* (1926) p. 269.

but the weak "crying out" of the soul against a destiny unsuccessfully resisted. Confession is not motivated by fear or consequences, for expediency only is born of fear. Rather, confession is the courage and willingness to face the consequences. It is not motivated by the desire for reward, for it is its own reward, unsought, and therefore complementary.

Confession is heroism of mind and will. The same power that brought the moral defeat is that which alone can achieve victory. There is no deception but self-deception, and confession is free of deceit. Confession restores the balance, it re-directs the forces within along channels that make for the benefit of the personality of all concerned. It re-baptizes the soul into a new life—free from self-interest, free from fear, free from falsehood. Through confession the Moral Law achieves the triumph of principles.

When Almayer felt the force of disastrous defeat, he wept over the body of the supposed Dain, wept for his own degradation, yet refusing to detach himself from those interests that caused it. Later when he stood with Nina and Dain, he was impelled for the moment to confess his shame and bless those two that had disrupted his plans—instead, he uttered his refusal to Nina to forgive her. Had he made that sweeping confession, blotting out the false moves of the past, revealing the deceit that had been in his heart, Almayer would have been at once ennobled in her eyes—but the moment passed, and the escape was gone forever.

Willems measured his degradation in the solitude of the forest, but instead of confessing to himself the cause of it, he rebuked the cruelty of Providence to which he ascribed his downfall. The attempt to blame others, to ascribe blame to circumstances, to Providence, was at once an acknowledgment of his guilt, and at the same time the revelation of his lack of heroism to face self-knowledge.

The Planter of Malata, on board his schooner, resolved

to confess his false play. The secret of his actions had had an innocent motive, but now, by its connection of content, a moral significance. His courage failed, he refused to struggle and fell, for "everything is possible except sincerity such as only stark struggling humanity can know."[42]

Freya and Allen both acknowledged the cause of their defeat, but neither yielded to the forces that would have made possible the realization of their hopes.

There was a ring of deepest sincerity in Kurtz final cry, in "The Heart of Darkness": "The Horror, the Horror." It was his confession. "After all, this was the expression of some sort of belief; it had candour, it had conviction, it had a vibrating note of revolt in its whisper, it had the appalling force of a glimpsed truth—the strange commingling of desire and hate."[43]

These are a few instances of the negative treatment of confession. On the positive side a few instances may suffice. Laughing Ann, in "Because of the Dollars," offers a form of confession that found no verbal expression. She was an outcast who had taken her last chance for the sake of her illegitimate boy. She lived with Bamtz, loafer and rascal. In the fight to murder Davidson in order to secure his shipment of money, Laughing Ann warned him and met thereby her own death. Davidson took the boy and sent him to a home. Her own unselfish interest in her boy had caused Davidson to trade with Bamtz, and her redeeming act fulfilled through him her hopes in the lad.

It was at the table with Marlow that Jim poured out his secret life to his guest. That confession exhibited to Marlow the real man, the hidden conflicts and sincere desire to redeem his past. The result was that Marlow secured a post for Jim, and in that far distant post, Jim found the oppor-

[42] *Within the Tides* (1925) p. 41.
[43] *Youth* (1925) p. 151.

tunity to undo the evil of the past and to reunite himself with his kind. There is a power in sincerity that makes itself felt. Jim's refusal that day to deceive himself offered the opportunity that otherwise would not have occurred. Marlow's interest in Jim, inspired by the latter's confession, gave Jim confidence in himself, and it was this single strand that served to reunite him with that community of interest whose trust he had unintentionally betrayed.

Arletta, in *The Rover,* had been restless and misanthropic since they had killed her father and mother when she was a little girl. She had been touched by the red hand of the Revolution and her feet "had run ankle-deep through the terrors of death."[44] She feared Scavola, she feared everyone save Peyrol, and lived in the strange and unwholesome solitude of her seared soul. She hated people. "Had they run away and left her she would not have thought of them at all."[45] Réal, shortly after he came to the farm, had unknowingly touched the finer side of her warped nature. Réal loved her, but "honor, decency, every principle forbade him to trifle with the feelings of a poor creature with her mind darkened by a very terrifying experience."[46] It was the presence of Réal that extended her interest beyond her darkened mind, and with the new contacts came a feeling of utter unworthiness. One day in the solitude of the Presbytery she uttered the secret misgivings of her heart and with the confession was lifted a great burden from her mind. Réal knew nothing of the drama enacting itself within the heart of Arletta, and though he witnessed a change in her behavior, he still thought of her as one whose feelings he would never know.

One day Arletta sought Réal in his room. Her voice and

[44] *The Rover* (1923) p. 260.
[45] *Ibid.* p. 161.
[46] *Ibid.* p. 209.

actions were different, but he bade her leave, and when she had gone, he flung himself upon the bed, burying his head in the pillow to stifle a cry for her return. He planned to go on the tartane against the English—it was to be the sacrifice of his own life for the good of Arletta. At the tartane, Peyrol was about to give the little boat over to Réal for the accomplishment of this purpose, when Arletta was discovered running toward them. Accusing Peyrol of taking Réal from her, she fell as one dead upon the deck. Peyrol saw and understood. Directing Réal to carry the unconscious girl back to the farm, the Old Rover felt something of a joy as he boarded the tartane and sailed away in Réal's stead.

Réal and Arletta, on different planes of life, found their inclusion in the society of their fellows when self was forgotten. Arletta's confession at the Presbytery, Réal's, in the form of silent and violent struggle, had prepared each for the appreciation of the other. The content given by that universal solidarity could not have been appropriated until the principles governing it were triumphant in their separate lives.

One of the most dramatic instances of the meaning of confession is traced by this master painter of human experience in his character, Razumov. From that moment of weakness, leading to his betrayal of Haldin, and the subsequent steps in the intricate pathways of falsehood, the cumulative force of Razumov's false career receives its release in that momentous hour of his heroic confession, undoing the evil of the past, and initiating the tragic character of the man into a new life of meaningful unfoldment.

Ambitious for recognition of conventional society, Razumov betrayed the anarchist, Haldin, to save himself. Haldin did not disclose Razumov's part in the betrayal at the trial of the former, and, consequently, Razumov was regarded by Haldin's associates as the latter's friend. This misunderstanding of the nature of Razumov's act was permitted by the latter to persist. At Geneva, the mother and sister of the unfortunate Haldin held Razumov in high esteem, and the revolutionists there took him into their confidence. He had been sent to Geneva as a spy by the Russian authorities. He was a victim of untoward circumstances, and his weakness drew him into a net that was woven, not by fate, but by the falsehoods that he had permitted and feared to unravel. When he discovered that Haldin had not disclosed his treachery, Razumov felt safe.

What was heinous in Razumov's deed? He had actually committed no crime. His silence violated the principles of the Moral Law. His betrayal of a revolutionist was born of selfish fear, and fear demanded expediency. It was not, therefore, a question whether the revolutionists were right or wrong in their political philosophy. The question was of moral import—falsehood, the inability to consider his relation with expansive goodness. He broke the bonds of that solidarity by his selfish act. He could not trust himself, because it was of himself that he was ever thinking.

To Miss Haldin he said: "There is in you no guile, no deception, no falsehood, no suspicion."[47] Thus in emphasizing the absence of those negative qualities in her character, he was pronouncing their presence in his own. He asked her if she believed in the efficacy of remorse, seeking in the struggle of his mind for some semblance of atonement. He thinks her the embodiment of that forgiveness that he desires, and in his obscure words, his illusions, and symbolic story of the betrayal, she understands. Later in his diary he wrote that it was she who was "appointed to undo the evil, making me betray myself back into truth and peace." That

[47] *Under Western Eyes* (1926) p. 349.

same night he confessed voluntarily to the company of revolutionists. "Today of all days since I came among you, I was made safe, and today I made myself free from falsehood, from remorse—independent of every single human being on this earth."[48]

This scene is one of the most dramatic in the novels of Conrad. Before his confession, Razumov was free from suspicion, and, now, with the confession, he was free from himself.

The brutal attack of the terrible Nikita, the accident caused by the tram car, rendering him an invalid for life, are incomparable in view of the great sufferings of the past. For the first time, sympathy is provoked for Razumov and his name among the revolutionists was elevated even above that of Haldin.

By that single act of heroic confession, Razumov linked himself once again to the society that he had injured. One may justify his previous conduct—but the feeling is quite different relative to his final heroism—that feeling is the kind that brings him into the circle of universal sympathy and understanding.

---

[48] *Ibid.* p. 368.

PART IV

HUMAN SOLIDARITY

I. RECAPITULATION

THE term "Human Solidarity" has been referred to throughout the treatment of Conrad's philosophy of life. It was necessary to refer to the notion from time to time, for it forms the basic postulate of his philosophy. It is implied throughout the range of Conrad's novels and serves both as a background and a concrete expression relative to the forces of the Moral Law. Before considering the contrast that our author implies between Human Solidarity and artificial institutions, it may be well to review the concept briefly.

The Cosmos is to be regarded as neutral stuff, so often referred to by Conrad as "the immensity of indifference." Out of this neutral stuff, man moulds the material of his experiences. Conrad does not distinguish carefully between the aspects of differences implied in his terminology. This is to be expected, for a work of art is not a logical demonstration, but an interpretation. Though the distinctions are vague, the difference between Human Solidarity and the bland Cosmos is clearly implied in the context of his writings. If one can conceive of Being without quality, without determinations, which receives through the forms of ideas a kind of "otherness," perhaps the effort will serve to illustrate Conrad's distinction. The Hegelian trilogy does not describe Conrad's position, rather, it illustrates the sameness and difference contained in these two terms. In a word, Human Solidarity is the *concretion* of the Cosmos. It is a reality of relations that finds activity through the Moral Law, the latter the Categorical Imperative of practical life.

Man's relation to that Reality is defined as one to a world of *selves,* which may be construed in terms of an Infinite Individual. This latter term is but the personification of Human Solidarity as opposed to the "finite self" or individual life. It is this Infinite Individual, past, present, and potential, that creates the connection-content, to borrow a term from Bosanquet, in which the "finite individual" discovers the significance of his existence and the value of his manifold relations.

The individual's relation to the wider context described is inescapable. It gives the content from which he selects, and determines the value of his choice. The selective processes of the individual, through his transmutation of experience, define a *logic* that is the law of progress, and at the same time the determinant of all valuations. The logic is imposed from without—which is to say, by Human Solidarity, the apparent dualism between the wider context and that of the individual being bridged by the Moral Law. This Law of Progress may further be defined as the universal, correcting force, and the ground of interpretative levels in relation to human life.

The apparent confusion of the Moral Law with the processes of rationalization is due to the fact that Conrad always regards such processes as of moral import. With him, without exception, progress is dispositional, a self-realization that connotes the realization of the Social Self.

In fine, the term "Human Solidarity" is a word that summarizes the meaning of the moral drama portrayed in his works. It represents true Reality, like the Platonic world of Ideas in which participation defines relations of infinite significance.

Separation from Human Solidarity is to be rendered an

outcast regardless of the integrity of one's relation to his immediate social environment; disobedience of its laws is to be crushed, for it is the blow, and at the same time, that which is stricken. It is that which warns and from which there is no escape; it is the Absolute Law from which codes receive their temporal significance, and human institutions, their meaning.

Human Solidarity may be symbolized by the "sense of mystery surrounding our lives" and "the latent feeling of fellowship with all creation—and to the subtle but invincible conviction of solidarity that knits together the loneliness of innumerable hearts to the solidarity in dreams, in joy, in sorrow, in aspiration, in illusions, in hope, in fear, which bind men to each other, which binds together all humanity—the dead to the living, and the living to the unborn."[1]

2. HUMAN SOLIDARITY, NOT ARTIFICIAL INSTITUTIONS

Human Solidarity is represented further through those particulars that may be described as "artificial institutions." This latter term serves to differentiate between "society" as the divine universal and the more concrete form as presented in temporary institutions. Artificial institutions represent codes, morals, customs, or levels of interpretation of Human Solidarity.

A code there must be—a code subjected, like all equipment of rationalization, to revision and modification. Codes or traditions represent a vicarious experience of the race and are, therefore, relative as compared with the absolute dictates of the Moral Law. When "authority" of the Moral Law is vested in forms of external authority, the relativity of the latter is necessary, for Truth is not static. In spite of

---

[1] *The Nigger of the "Narcissus"* (1918) p. viii f.

this relativity, as represented by the codes and traditions of artificial institutions, there cannot be anarchistic abandonment, for the refutation of these traditions requires a code. So it follows that artificial institutions represent levels of interpretation, but do not, collectively, offer a substitute for Human Solidarity.

Razumov was a social outcast and "he was as lonely in the world as a man swimming in the deep sea. The word Razumov was a mere label of a solitary individuality."[2] That is why Haldin appeared to be an obstruction to Razumov's ambition, for the anarchistic abandonment of the latter disturbed the harmony of the sense of organized society. To Razumov, the present artificial institutions "appeared to him rational and . . . had a force of harmony in contrast with the horrible discord in this man's presence."[3] Razumov's methods employed to eliminate Haldin violated the principles of Human Solidarity, for his hate, distrust, and cruelty destroyed the very conditions that made conscious inclusion within society possible. Here Conrad has exhibited the difference between the two terms and likewise their intimate relations.

After Razumov betrayed Haldin, he returned to his unsuspecting prisoner. The very words of Haldin, friendly and innocent, were replete with sinister suggestions to Razumov as they were distilled through the fear-intoxicated mind of the listener. The underhand means that Razumov used to "honor" the protective power of society was the sacrifice of those qualities that were necessary for inclusion. The sacrifice was not the loss of those things labelled by Razumov —fame, important connections, popularity—but the sacrifice of that "something" within that made him a moral outcast. To have declared his true position relative to Haldin

[2] *Under Western Eyes* (1926) p. 10.
[3] *Ibid.* p. 21.

would not have involved Razumov's life, as the story well implies, while the willingness to make such a sacrifice would not have necessitated the moral stress that occurred. This distinction is made more clear in the following instances.

Hervey, in "The Return," was a successful business man. He felt himself to be an important factor in conventional society. His materialism grew out of the effort to entrench himself more securely in the protecting interests of artificial institutions. It was "self" that Hervey was interested in, and his unconscious emphasis upon self-interest rendered the tangibles of life more and more meaningless. When he realized the true significance of existence, those things that he had held essential became empty and void—and in the moment of that self-realization "he felt his fellowship with every man."

It is to be observed in passing that the Moral Law is a correcting force, and that moral stress is necessitated by the degree of that which requires correction. Tragedies are not difficulties, for these are never motiveless, but in the refusal to sacrifice self-interest for the benefit of the larger. If man would only recognize in the "oppositions" and conflicts of life a call to larger significance, a call to come up higher, he would catch more clearly the meaning of living.

In "A Smile of Fortune," the relativity of social forces is exhibited in contrast with the Absolute Authority of the Moral Law as expressed in Human Solidarity. The first Jacobus was a social outcast, the second, held in high esteem. The captain was surprised at this, because of the humaneness of the first, the misanthropy of the second. Convention, in its regard for wealth, had reversed the order of intrinsic rank. Conrad has here touched upon a frequent condition in society, allowing as he does, for the relative force of conventional authority, and its correction necessitating a higher context as the ground of judgment. Here, the semblance of the social force and relative permanence too often hides the broken bonds of that true society of which it is representative. One Jacobus sinned against the human laws, the other, against the Moral. In a word, all externalities of life, represented in the accepted codes of action, must enhance the conditions that make for the solidarity of universal fellowship, for only at those significant points in which the Moral Law operates, does man contact the Reality at his elbow.

No one can be indifferent to the relation between the codes of life and Human Solidarity. Heyst in *Victory* was a victim of "the great joke." "Is there no guidance?" he asked his father. "You still believe in something then?" his father scornfully replied. "You believe in flesh and blood perhaps. A full and equable contempt would soon do away with that, too. But since you have not attained it, I advise you to cultivate that form of contempt which is called pity. It is perhaps the least difficult—always remembering that you, too, if you are anything, are as pitiable as the rest, yet never expecting any pity for yourself."[4] The attempt to isolate one's self, to become immune to conflict is to lose contact with the principles of life, it is to be solitary and lonely. Pity was the one strand that united Heyst with his kind and finally brought him to his realization.

Decound, in *Nostromo,* exercised a different kind of indifference. He was a materialist and cynic, and his habits induced in him "a mere barren indifferentism passing as intellectual superiority."[5] Later Nostromo found the lighter empty and floating near the shore, the one that he had left on the island for Decound. Where was Decound? Decound alone knew. He had died from solitude "a victim of the disillusioned weariness which is the retribution meted out to

---

[4] *Victory* (1925) p. 194.
[5] *Nostromo* (1928) p. 152.

intellectual audacity." The "brilliant Don Decound, weighted by the bars of San Tomé silver, disappeared without a trace, swallowed up in the immense indifference of things."[6]

The significance of Human Solidarity must be discovered through one's conscious activity. Neither indifference, on the one hand, nor complacent trust in artificial institutions, on the other, will suffice. As Powell, in *Chance,* remarked regarding the complacency of the people about him: "They see, that no matter what they do this tight little island won't turn turtle with them or spring a leak and go to the bottom with their wives and children."[7] So felt Marlow when he returned to the city after his hallowing experiences in Africa. "Their bearing, which was simply the bearing of commonplace individuals going about their business in the assurance of perfect safety, was an offence to me, like the outrageous flauntings of folly in the force of a danger it is unable to comprehend."[8]

The professor, in *The Secret Agent,* had had ambitions. He sought personal power and position and the social order failed to appreciate his merits as he represented them. Then the professor exercised a ruthless defiance against the artificial institutions. He carried a time detonator in his pocket. He had but to press the button and he would be no more. This gave him an enormous feeling of importance. ". . . in their own way the most ardent of revolutionaries are perhaps doing no more but seeking for peace in common with the rest of mankind—the peace of soothed vanity, of satisfied appetites, or perhaps of appeased conscience. . . ."[9] Separated from the community of common interests, the forces that might have held them together brought them

[6] *Ibid.* p. 501.
[7] *Chance* (1924) p. 4.
[8] *Youth* (1925) p. 152.
[9] *The Secret Agent* (1927) p. 81.

low in the dust of ignominy. Against the content given by Human Solidarity, they grappled for the same under another name.

If the present arrangement of social organization is faulty, it is not adjusted through personal abandonment, for artificial institutions, like finite individuals, have their ground in Human Solidarity. They are concrete expressions of the present level of advancement, an advancement subject to correction, but not to abandonment. Therefore these revolutionists in separating themselves from the community of common interests, grappled for the same interests under selfish forms. One may liken artificial institutions to the *Narcissus* upon the lonely sea. It represents the tangible expression of the crew's need of fellowship. Mutiny would be disastrous to that fellowship.

In "An Outpost of Progress," some three hundred miles from the nearest trading station, Kayert, Carlier had been placed by their superiors. With these two white men was Makola, who could think, and ten lazy negroes who feigned assistance in menial tasks. These two white men were "two perfectly insignificant and incapable individuals, whose existence is only rendered possible through the high organization of civilized crowds. Few men realize that their life, the very essence of their character, their capabilities, and their audacities, are only the expression of their belief in the safety of their surroundings."[10] These two mechanized individuals were robbed of their audacity when removed from the safety of their former surroundings. They feared the power of public opinion; they feared the solitude into which destiny had ruthlessly thrust them. They were drawn to one another at this outpost because of fear. They talked like brothers, because, far from the supporting props of civilization, they were afraid to be alone. Society had

[10] *Tales of Unrest* (1926) p. 89.

robbed them of independent thought, the ability to confront the unusual, not intentionally, but because its needs required routine work, and these two were able to fulfil that need. Out there in the freedom of open spaces, away from the restrictions of convention, these two white men were in bondage—slaves of their feebleness. When the unusual confronted them in the form of menacing savages, they were confused, but Makola, who could think, mastered the situation—for himself. Later, in a personal quarrel, one was shot, the other, hopelessly distracted, sought the grave of another white man who had died before their arrival in this desolate country. As Kayert lay dying upon the grave, the whistle of a steamer broke the silence. It was the return of the Director—but too late. "Society was calling to its accomplished child to come, to be taken care of, to be instructed, to be judged, to be condemned."[11]

The principle is expressed, from another point of view in "The Duel," in the incident when Feraud and D'Hubert were drawn to one another during the Moscow retreat. It was a moment when the support of society had been withdrawn and the *felt-need* of coöperation presented itself. Also, in "Gaspar Ruiz," in the absence of artificial institutions, torn asunder by revolution, the force of Human Solidarity was contacted in a strange manner. Ruiz had not the power of mind to accomplish his destiny—he was inert mentally, but deeply sympathetic. The girl had the will and mind, but lacked sympathy. His mind was stimulated by her will, and her spirit was governed by his sympathy.

In the two latter tales, conditions were favorable in the form of reënforcement of character, while in the case of "An Outpost of Progress," the removal of support left the two white men helpless because of lack of personal force. Society does support and give content in proportion to its

[11] *Ibid.* p. 116.

level of representation of Human Solidarity, but as a means to the strengthening of dispositional qualities. Society cannot offer a substitute for individual self-attainment.

3. HUMAN SOLIDARITY, NOT TO BE CONSTRUED ANTHROPOMORPHICALLY

Just as artificial institutions reflect a level of interpretation, so may morals and the idea of God, as commonly accepted, serve as points of contact. Likewise, as with social codes, of which these form a part, an anthropomorphic conception of God cannot be offered as a substitute for the Moral Law, or annul the force of the latter as represented by Human Solidarity.

Conrad does not explicitly treat of religious conceptions, yet implicitly defines man as a religious animal. The notion connoted by the term "religion" may be defined, as far as Conrad is concerned, as embracing life and man's moral relation to it. Religion is an *individual* affair, that is to say, dispositional. It is always dispositional in content and expresson. No ritualistic exercise can substitute for religion as Conrad appears to conceive it. It is an individual affair because it is a universal matter.

The world is organized for man's good, which is to say, for the good of all. That organization has its levels of interpretation ever in relation to that "ghostly reality." The intricate connection-content that describes the whole in which the individual context is a part, is discovered through those moral stresses, those self-tested experiences, out of which emerges the meaning of human experience. The moral drama of life, as symbolized in the works of Conrad, well illustrates this. To violate the principles that keep true Human Solidarity intact is not only tragic for the individual, but for those, innocent as they may be, who are allied with the offender, for the mesh of relations, like the spider's web, must feel the force of one destroyed thread.

The spiritual values given by Human Solidarity, discovered through moral stress, and attained in the triumph of principles, is a consideration basic to the appreciation of the whole range of Conrad's thought. In view of this principle, it follows, as already reiterated, that artificial institutions, no matter how representative these may be in their manifold codes, cannot offer a substitution for that form of inner activity in which one alone is capable of triumph. Artificial institutions, likewise, have their content given by that reality connoted in the term Human Solidarity.

Life is an individual affair. It is a case of being instrumental merely, or a conscious agent in the exercise of cosmic forces, that is, to employ the Conradian expression—whether one believes simply in the safety of his surroundings, or whether one trusts in life. The first is acquiescence, like Kayert and Carlier who were rendered inefficient by their belief in the protecting influences of society; the second, like Lord Jim in his final triumph, or Lingard, whose accomplishment was the result of self-attainment, free of external support, unspoiled in his greatness.

The Outcast of the islands blamed Providence for his downfall and wondered at its neglect relative to his selfish ambitions. Jean-Pierre turned to the Church, an externality for him, for some magic power to ward off an evil spell. Power lay within—both disregarded its source. Their respective hardships were due to lack of conformity with the interests of the "divine society," and each interpreted his hardships as expressive of the cruelty of life. Each refused to see that cruelty, alleged, as something benevolent in its proffered opportunities for wrestling the real gain in life. The Outcast stumbled and knew why he fell, for he argued against those whisperings within that represented the conviction of right direction.

Indeed, who would not choose a life of struggle and difficulties, where victory emerges finally from a thousand failures, rather than Willems' preferred world in which tragic reliance could gain nothing permanent, or Bessie's prosaic existence where there was no gold because there was no refining process.

Many of the characters in Conrad's novels lose the significance of meaningful life through wilful resistance, a few, on the other hand, because of an apparent immunity relative to the resistive forces of life, and one or two tales reflect a tragic result due to unconscious substitution of an externality for the Moral Law.

In "The End of the Tether," is noted a dependence upon an anthropomorphic conception of God. It is one of the most interesting of tales from the pen of Conrad from this point of view.

The noble captain triumphed, but he did not know it. He exercised those qualities that brought him into contact with the principles of Human Solidarity, but he failed to realize it. He brought his noble career to a premature end because he thought himself a failure. He did not realize the benevolence of Providence because his anthropomorphism did not discover it.

His conception of God, instead of being a regulative principle in his thinking was an "object" to which he created a false attachment. Conrad, it is to be remembered, is not rebuking any conception of God, but rather he is taking issue with the substitution of that conception for the Moral Law. The Moral Law never fails, as this tale in common with others illustrates, though one's conception of Providence may meet with disappointment. How often when things go well, we emphasize our achievement, and when things go awry, we question the will of God. There is an inconsistency in such that accounts somewhat for the tragedy of discouragement.

Captain Whalley, in "The End of the Tether," at sixty-seven years of age, was not leading a desirable or enterprizing existence on his monotonous round of sixteen hundred miles. He had been famous in his day as a captain and had accumulated a fortune. Then his ample competence was lost through the crash of the Decan Banking Corporation. He had buried his devoted wife at sea. His little daughter had grown to womanhood, married and journeyed to a distant city to live. Her husband became an invalid. When Whalley lost his fortune, his daughter unaware of her father's misfortune, requested aid. Whalley had retained his little barque, *Fair Maid*. When his daughter wrote of her difficulties, Whalley sold the barque and from the proceeds forwarded to her the amount that she requested. He was now left, unknown to her, without a home and almost destitute. His faith in God was firm, and Whalley prayed that he might discover other means of helping her.

That means came when Whalley was appointed captain of the *Sofala*. Though the owner was a gambler, and the steamer unattractive, Whalley accepted the partnership. Through this means he prayed that he might be enabled to continue his assistance to his daughter and be prevented from being a burden to her.

One day, near the end of Whalley's tenure of office, the *Sofala* docked at the jetty in front of Van Wyk's bungalow. Whalley accepted Van Wyk's invitation to dinner. At the table, that which the mate Sterne had discovered some time ago, was made known to Van Wyk. Old Captain Whalley was going blind, and his old Serang, ever at his side, was Whalley's "eyes." This return trip was to be the last after leaving Van Wyk, and the contract with Massy, the owner, would be honored. There would be enough money for his daughter. Whalley prayed that his blindness might not be discovered.

As the steamer left the jetty and steamed out toward the reefs, Massy, ignorant of Whalley's defect, decided to wreck the *Sofala* in order to secure the insurance money. Filling his jacket with iron weights, Massy hung it unobserved near the compass to deflect the magnetic needle. The Serang read the compass indications to Whalley—and the steamer struck the reefs.

Captain Whalley refused to leave the sinking steamer. He felt that his God had forsaken him, and finding the jacket with its iron weights, put it on and disappeared with the steamer in the depths of the sea.

This noble soul believed firmly in the beneficence of Providence. When he knew that his eyesight was failing, he continued his evoking of divine assistance. When, at last, blindness shut from view the world of his usefulness, and the ship struck the reefs, from what he believed to be a fault of his, his resignation was supreme.

Conrad illustrates the problem here of that cry of the ages, "My God, why hast thou forsaken me?" His treatment of this problem is not a disparagement of faith in God, for the perspective has always given the answer.

Did God forsake this noble soul? That his soul was noble proves not. Whalley is not impressed upon our consideration because he was the captain of that unfortunate steamer, nor because he went blind. Rather he lives in our admiration because of the reason *why* he was captain, and for his heroic efforts in behalf of another. These fine principles that represent Human Solidarity, when they find expression in man, represent all that men feel when they say "God." His prayer was answered, for he found himself in his sacrifice for another. The blind beggar may solicit our sympathy, or self-pity, but the blindness of Whalley is forgotten in the light of his heroic soul. The steamer and Whalley's affliction become instruments of interest because associated with his heroism.

The beneficence of Providence is judged according to the individual's conception of it, hence, the individual judgment is often disappointed—though the Moral Law never fails. The enigma of Divine Justice is not solved in human concepts, but in those intangible successes of triumphant life. "It is made clear through sacrifice."

Witness Lord Jim striving to mend the results of his violation of trust in his kind; recall Karain in his defeated life, holding the desired tangible in his feeble grasp; remember Nostromo, proud in his trustworthiness, despairing under the weight of his unintentional theft; see Whalley and Peyrol going down beneath the merciless waves in their supreme sacrifice for others. The enigma is solved only in the wrestling with the forces that make for the good. Man's conditions and accidents are the hieroglyphics to be solved in heroic discipline.

The Moral Law has a literal and a spiritual interpretation. The letter of the Law is represented in those codes and symbols of artificial institutions, and, likewise, in various conceptions of God. These serve as a guide and a direction, and as such are indispensable. The spirit of the Law is revealed in that inward activity that represents the real drama of human life. It is by the latter alone that individual character either attains what it ought to be, or is crushed by the recoil of outraged nature.

The particular and practical question is this. What matters it whether one believes or not in the safety of his surroundings, or whether one puts his *trust* in life? In the first, life seems cruel, disappointments are the results of struggle, gain has little or no meaning, and life is empty and without peace. In the second, such a trust discovers one's true relationship with that which gives true value; hardships are transmuted into hope, faith, and honest endeavor, and disappointments become simply episodes in the drama of final triumph. To rest upon the first is to increase the uncertainty within, to trust in the second is to lose that uncertainty in the discovery of the permanent. That is to say, to do what is felt to be right, because it requires no argument, no self-justification, is peace, is happiness, is answered prayer, and the reward of faith in God.

4. SUMMUM BONUM

The highest good may easily be inferred from the negative treatment in Conrad's novels, and, in a few instances, from the examples of triumphant life.

Triumphant life is not to be judged by the possession of tangibles, nor by those achievements usually deemed by the world as indicative of success. Success or victory is defined by Conrad in terms of character, or self-realization, all that re-unites man with his kind and fulfills thereby the purpose of the Moral Law. On the other hand, Conrad does not imply that the possession of tangibles, success in the attainment of one's desires are opposed to triumphant life—in fact, it is not a question of possession at all, but whether self-interest, in any of its manifold forms, results in self-defeat, thwarting the purpose of the Moral Law. The purpose of the Moral Law is the fulfillment of the interest of the Infinite Individual.

Conrad does not define the ultimate purpose of the Moral Law save in terms of individual realization which, again, is always to be understood in terms of the social individual. The very fact that any action that violates the relation of man to Human Solidarity robs the objects of true content argues the purpose of that Law.

The drama of human experience so skillfully and subtly painted and traced by this master hand, exhibits the reiterated emphasis upon the good of the Moral Law. His examples of the evil resulting from the refusal to wrestle the gain offered by the indifferent Cosmos is an argument in the negative. The Moral Law operates whether man obeys it or not. He may trifle, he may push his own self-interest to the fore—but only to discover with Willems that Providence is unkind and unjust, that is, relative to his own notion of what is good. Kurtz, with his ivory, Hervey, with his social ambitions, Nostromo, with his unwanted silver—how empty were these severally achieved ambitions. Failing to relate one's inward activity with the Law of human relations, the very notions of justice and contentment become empty, and with these the benevolent Power of the Moral Law is objectified and personified in fatalistic terms. This is the tragedy of separation.

Heyst and Decound rightly construed the nothingness of the Cosmos. Their respective errors lay in their conception of their relation to that indifference. But even this element of error was an opportunity, for even failure to find meaning in any particular notion of it is an advanced step. Decound stopped with the illusion, Heyst transmuted its negativity into terms of positive significance.

The secret of life is hidden by unconcern. Travers and Bessie remained untouched. One sailed away in his luxurious yacht self-satisfied and proud, the other simply existed in her prosaic surroundings indifferent and immuned to conflict.

Lord Jim represents one of the finest examples of genuine triumph. Like Heyst and Kurtz, the victory came late, but, nevertheless, a victory. Though it is possible to conceive of an interchange of circumstances in the case of these three characters, the end would have been the same—for their respective triumphs were dispositional, not circumstantial.

Jim, through his resistance of fear and selfishness, forced his ideas of peace and unity upon the community at Patusan. When, finally, the scoundrel Brown visited the island and injected his poison into the minds of Jim's tribe, Jim was unafraid. It was not safe for him to go out among his people. Jim did go out. He went straight to the council and there met his death at the hands of Doramin, unflinching—victoriously. The gain wrestled from the dumb Cosmos is obtained only through the same principles that make that gain possible in idea. Jim had dreamed of great things, of courage, of strength, of sacrifice. When the conditions within were fulfilled, his dreams found victorious actuality.

The lateness of the triumphs in the lives of these characters has given a pessimistic cast to the thought of Conrad. That view of Conrad, however, argues the ground upon which he has based his optimism. He has shown that "settled convictions," "secret fears," "false attachments" are the conditions that create barriers to self-realization. Self-realization is the only form of triumph, for through it alone the meaningful relations with that which gives true value and content are discovered. Self-defeat, in the presence of the tangibles desired and possessed, argues that triumph does not lie in self-interest. The lateness of triumph, therefore, is due to the conditions within that must be fulfilled before life unfolds in meaning.

Conrad's very dualism discovers a unity that forbids personal detachment. In that unity man becomes a part of the living tissue of that wider context, Human Solidarity. Within it, man has lost somewhat his imputed greatness, for his greatness is the realization of the social self. Man is not minimized in this moral scheme because true manhood discovers its meaning as a norm in that wider context.

Take Razumov, for an example, he does not loom large in one's regard until he has disentangled himself from the web of personal interests and individual ambitions, until in heroic self-forgetfulness he stands out in true individuality. That Travers fades into insignificance in the presence of Lingard is not given in the external circumstances respectively attached to each. Every character that impresses itself upon the reader's sympathetic interest, does so in proportion as each successfully struggles with the natural impediments to self-realization.

The highest good is realization of the social self, for the unity of life is described in a context of which each individual is part. The world is not cruel, but is the "best possible world," for it meets the conditions that afford the individual his opportunity for growth, and rebukes the stagnation of selfish ambitions that would separate him from the reward of true manhood.

The Moral Law is absolute, and for that reason creates the misadjustments and confusions of every age—for like the fire that burns, its rigidity is the ground of its utilization. It renders possible the attainment of those qualities that alone can meet the demands of mind and will in the satisfaction of the good—morally, intellectually, and socially.

Self-realization—"Droll thing life is—that mysterious arrangement of merciless logic for a futile purpose. The most you can hope from it is some knowledge of yourself."[12] That is the real gain in life—that inexplicable something that "holds us together."

It is most fitting that the unfinished novel of Conrad, *Suspense,* stops with Cosmo sailing away with Attilio. To what port he came we do not know, but his will was strong, his hands, clean. In one of the great crises of his life he did not falter under the stress of the moment. He lost Adéle,

[12] *Youth* (1925) p. 150.

but gained his freedom and left intact the strands that bound him to the community of his kind. "It's the idea," after all, and it is there that the real life is to be found—or lost forever. It was that that spelled the fated position of his star, and put the other members of the constellation in darkness —unnoticed and unwanted.

Such appears to be Conrad's philosophy of life as reflected in his novels. In his note to *Chance,*[13] Conrad has summarized the purpose of his work, the fulfillment of which his gifted pen has played so splendid a part:

> "It may have happened to me to sin against taste now and then, but apparently I have never sinned against the basic feelings and elementary convictions which make life possible to the mass of mankind, and, by establishing a standard of judgment, set their idealism free to look for the plainer ways, for higher feelings, for deeper purposes."

[13] *Chance* (1924) p. xii.

THE END

LIST OF NOVELS AND TALES OF JOSEPH CONRAD ALLUDED TO IN THE TEXT

Arrow of Gold, The
Almayer's Folly
Chance
Falk
including the following tales:
"Falk"
"Amy Foster"
"To-Morrow"
Lord Jim
Mirror of the Sea, The
Nigger of the "Narcissus," The
Nostromo
Outcast of the Islands, An
Personal Record, A
Rescue, The
Rover, The
Secret Agent, The
Set of Six, A
including the following tales:
"Gaspar Ruiz"
"The Informer"
"The Brute"
"An Anarchist"
"The Duel"
"Il Conde"
Shadow Line, The
Suspense

Tales of Unrest
including the following tales:
"Karain: A Memory"
"The Idiots"
"An Outpost of Progress"
"The Return"
"The Lagoon"
'Twixt Land and Sea
including the following tales:
"A Smile of Fortune"
"The Secret Sharer"
"Freya of the Seven Isles"
Typhoon
Under Western Eyes
Victory
Within the Tides
including the following tales:
"The Planter of Malata"
"The Partner"
"The Inn of the Two Witches"
"Because of the Dollars"
Youth
including the following tales:
"Youth"
"The Heart of Darkness"
"The End of the Tether"